INSTANT PIANO

INSTANT

PIANO

by Les Horan
and Linda Ekblad

St. Martin's Press
New York

ISBN 0-312-41875-2

First Edition

10 9 8 7 6 5 4 3 2 1

Acknowledgments

Many people helped with *Instant Piano,* but two people were crucial to its development. Special thanks are owed to Jaimie Newman for his words and ideas, and to Bill McCabe for his compositions and arrangements.

The music on the tape was recorded at Grand Slam Studios in West Orange, New Jersey, and One Right Angle Studio in New York City. Keyboards were played by Bill McCabe and Les Horan. Thanks to the following musicians: George Andrews, Glenn Rhian, Steve Bill, Dave Katzenberg, Seth Glassman, Ed Covi, Ronnie Kahn, and Bob Kindred.

INSTANT PIANO

Contents

Chapter 1
Join the Band

As the lights go up, the band runs onto the stage. The crowd roars, rattling the rafters. The drummer clicks off the beat with his sticks, the guitar player unleashes a thunderous chord, and the music suddenly explodes, like the finale of a Fourth of July fireworks display.

The big, thumping beat grabs you. You close your eyes, losing yourself in the sound and see ... *yourself,* on stage, pounding the keyboard, playing as though your life depended on it, laughing and shouting ...

And then, as you open your eyes, you think, "Forget it! I'll never be able to do that. It takes *years* to learn to play."

Get ready for an exciting surprise. In no time at all you're going to *be* part of the band, making real music with real musicians, having a ball. And there's not a single thing you have to know or do to be prepared.

- You don't have to read music.
- You don't have to practice or take lessons.
- You don't have to know about chords or scales.

So how on earth are you gonna do it? It's simple. With the special music of the *Instant Piano* tape and the hints in this book:

- You're going to sound like you've been playing for years, even if you've never touched a keyboard before!
- You're going to play immediately—not in weeks or months or years from now, but right away, the moment you begin!

When you turn on the tape that comes with this book, you'll hear many different kinds of music, from futuristic funk to light, lazy love songs. There's up-to-the-minute rock 'n' roll, old-fashioned doo-wop, low-down-and-dirty boogie-woogie, cool jazz, and red-hot rhythm and blues. The music on the tape swings. Some of it rocks, and some of it will make you want to dance. As good as it is, however, if you listen carefully, you'll notice it's missing the most important ingredient of any musical piece. You are going to provide that missing element!

You're the Star

■ Imagine a performance of a Beethoven violin concerto with everything but the violin. Imagine "You Are the Sunshine of My Life" without Stevie Wonder singing. Or how about the *1812* Overture without the cannons blasting away? Think about a world in which music consists entirely of accompaniments—supporting backgrounds—without lead singers or screaming guitar solos—without melodies.

The pieces you hear on the *Instant Piano* tape are part of that world. There are no lead singers or guitar solos. The songs on the tape have no melodies. They are accompaniments only, backgrounds, the music that supports Itzhak Perlman's violin or Stevie Wonder's magnificent pipes.

That's where you come in. You're going to be the star, the person who really makes the music happen, the one who steps out in front of the band and leads the way. You're going to fill in the solo, the missing melody.

Improvisation

■ Imagine a saxophone player stepping up to the microphone to play a solo in a smoky, sultry nightclub. He begins slowly, gently, thinking, listening, his fingers sightlessly scanning the keys of his horn, searching for just . . . the . . . right . . . note. When he first gets up to play, he probably has no idea of what exactly will happen when he sets the reed of his instrument to vibrating. He's *improvising*—making up the melody as he goes along. As the band grooves and simmers in the background, he starts cooking on the front burner, giving himself to the moment's inspiration. Before long, he's wailing and squalling, notes tumbling urgently from the upturned bell of his horn.

When you improvise, you're not playing a set tune, one that's been prepared in advance and written out for you to play. There's no special melody, no song to copy, no sounds in particular you're expected to reproduce. Instead, you just listen to the music in the background and play whatever notes turn up—you let your fingers do the walking.

The trick to improvising is getting your spontaneously generated melody to sound good with the accompaniment provided by the rest of the band. Usually, a jazz musician does this by knowing what key the music is in, which chords are being played, and which scales can be used against them. With *Instant Piano,* however, you are being spared these difficult details and can begin improvising melodies . . . instantly. By following one simple rule, you can immediately begin playing along with the *Instant Piano* tape—and we guarantee that your playing will sound great!

Stay on the Black Keys

■ What's the secret? Just this: When you play along with Side 1 of the *Instant Piano* tape, play only on the black keys of the piano. That's all there is to it! We've arranged the music on Side 1 in such a way that, no matter which black key you hit, and no matter where in a piece you hit it, the note you play will sound good and fit right in. Incredible as it sounds,

YOU CAN'T MAKE A MISTAKE IF
YOU STAY ON THE BLACK KEYS.

Getting Started

■ There's no one way to begin playing with *Instant Piano.* Some people approach it like certain swimmers approach the

ocean—first the big toe, then the entire foot up to the ankle . . .
slo-o-o-o-wly up the calves to the knees . . . now to the belly . . .
Others approach it like those who simply strip off their clothes,
remove their sunglasses, and before you can shout "Undertow!"
plunge headlong into the sheer face of a ten-foot swell.

As you begin to improvise with the tape, proceed at *your*
own pace, whatever feels comfortable to you. But if you'd like a
few hints on how to get started, we're happy to provide them.

Try This

1. Take a few deep breaths and shake your arms and
hands. Get loose. Relax.
2. Turn on Side 1 of the tape. You will hear a note
repeated several times. Play the note on your piano as you
hear the tape.

Play this note.

Do the notes sound the same? If they do, your piano is in
tune. If they are slightly different, you will still be able to
play along—your ear will adjust and not hear the difference after a few seconds.

If the note on the tape sounds very different from the note you are playing, however, either your piano needs to be tuned or your tape deck is running too fast or slow. If you are using an electronic keyboard, synthesizer, or electric organ, you probably have a knob you can turn to tune the instrument. If you are using an acoustic piano, you'll need to call a professional tuner. If you think the problem is your tape deck, check the batteries before bringing it into a shop to be fixed.

3. Adjust the volume when the music begins. Be sure you can hear both the recorded music and the sound of your own playing.

4. Listen to the accompaniment. Sit back and enjoy it. Tap your feet, hum along, get up and dance if you're moved to do so. Give yourself a chance to feel the music.

5. When you've gotten into the groove, play a black note, any black note. At first, you might be better off sticking to the notes on the right-hand side of the keyboard.

6. Play another black note. Listen to it. Compare its sound to the first. Then play another note. And another. Don't imagine that there are some notes you *should* be playing. Just let the sound of the music you play and hear lead you and carry you along.

7. If you are new to the piano, play single notes, one at a time. You might find it easier to play with one finger.

8. Keep your playing simple. You don't have to cram a million notes into each second of music. Play a note, play another note, rest a bit, play a few more, rest a bit . . .

9. Follow this simple formula in all your playing: *If*

what you're doing sounds good and feels good, keep doing it; if it doesn't, stop and try something else.

The above suggestions are *only* suggestions, intended simply to get you started. The only three instructions you really need for Side 1 are:

1. Turn on the tape.
2. Listen.
3. Play along using only the black notes.

Play Now, Read Later

■ That's all there is to it. You can put this book down right now, put the *Instant Piano* tape into your tape player, turn up the volume, and begin making music this very minute, without any further preparation. In fact, you never need to pick up this book again.

"So why then is there a book?" you might well ask.

Easy. We suspect that, after having spent some time jamming with the *Instant Piano* tape, you'll want to know more about making music. You'll want to *do* more, to make more music, and to make it *better*. In the rest of the book, we'll show you how to do just that—to turn your good playing into *great* playing. We'll introduce you to a wide variety of piano tricks and techniques—the nitty-gritty business of music-making—and we'll do it painlessly, without the burden of complicated music theory, note-reading, unfamiliar jargon, hours of boring drill, or memorization by rote. And, of course, we'll show you how to play along with Side 2 of the *Instant Piano* tape, using the *white keys* of the piano.

In the meantime:

> **The crowd is roaring. Searchlights sweep the hall. The music crashes over you like pounding surf. You close your eyes, lost in the sound, and you see . . . yourself, onstage, tearing into a screaming solo, the band urging you on, spotlights bearing down on you with the intensity of a thousand suns.**

Go join the band.

Chapter 2

Tapping into Your Creativity

Instant Piano is designed to allow people with no previous musical experience to participate immediately in the making of serious, expressive music—without lessons, without hours of practice, without any technical knowledge of music whatsoever. Simply by following a few easy guidelines, and listening carefully with your ears and your heart, you can penetrate instantly the seeming mysteries of music-making. You can begin shaping your own melodies, inventing your own harmonies, telling your own stories, baring your own soul in sound.

If you have followed the instructions in the first chapter and have begun playing along with the *Instant Piano* tape, you have already discovered some of the possibilities for self-expression it provides. To get the most out of *Instant Piano*, however, we've included a few more simple suggestions.

Get Silly

■ A good way to approach *Instant Piano* is playfully, the way children approach games with one another. Prepare yourself to be silly, reckless, unguarded, joyous, and carefree. Place that stuffy adult judge aside. A few ways to warm up at the keyboard are given here. They are designed to help you unwind and become playful.

1. Don't put on the tape. Instead, go to the piano and play it in the most raucous way you can think of.

2. Play with your elbows, your feet, the palms of your hands, your fists, your ears. Play as if you were a terrible two-year-old.

3. Play the sound your piano would make hitting the ground after falling forty stories.

4. Use your forearms, or a ruler, to play as many notes at one time as you possibly can.

5. Play using the eraser ends of two pencils, one pencil in each hand. Play like a four-year-old and, at the same time, sing a nonsense song. Make up the words and melody as you go—the way a four-year-old would.

6. Later, whenever you're playing with the *Instant Piano* tape and you feel your playing is growing stale, stop what you are doing and come back to these warm-up exercises. They're guaranteed to help free the child within.

Keep It Simple

■ A sad but unavoidable truth is that learning takes time. We learn in steps that often seem unbearably small. No one has ever sat down at a piano and, without having played a note before, found him- or herself able to play like Rubinstein or Oscar Peterson. Instead, each player must first learn and master very simple things. Ever so slowly the simple things become more complex. There's no jumping ahead, no way to force the process.

No matter what your level, you learn best by tackling easy tasks first.

The moral of all this is clear: As you play your way through *Instant Piano,* keep your playing simple. Do only what comes easily and naturally. If you push yourself too far beyond the level of your actual ability, you'll begin to tighten up, tense up, and enjoy yourself a lot less. And when you do, you'll find that much less learning takes place. When you reach this point, ease up. Don't punish yourself by repeatedly attempting to do what you *wish* you were able to do. And keep in mind that there is no necessary relationship between beauty and complexity. Some of the most beautiful things are the most simple. The jazz pianist Thelonious Monk once devastated a nightclub audience with a solo that consisted of just one note. You can't get much simpler than that!

Try This

1. Pick two, three, or four black notes anywhere on the keyboard. Play along with the tape using only those pre-selected notes. See how much variety you can create simply by varying the order in which they're played and the speed you use to play them.

2. Play using only the black notes on the bottom of the keyboard, or only those on the top third.

3. With your left hand, play only the lowest five black notes on the piano. With your right hand, play only the five highest.

4. Play holding each note you hit until the sound dies away.

Let Yourself Make Mistakes

■ Although the music on the *Instant Piano* tape was designed to make your playing mistake-proof, a few things can still go wrong. Your finger might miss the black note you aimed for and wind up instead scoring a direct hit on a horrible-sounding white note. You might lose the beat and feel helpless as your melody drifts off into rhythmic limbo. You might find yourself unable to actually execute, to your satisfaction, an astonishingly brilliant musical idea. Or, once executed, you might find that your stroke of genius was really a wretched dud.

When mistakes happen, do as the pros do—keep cool, keep smiling, keep playing as if nothing had happened. Quickly forget about whatever mistake you made. Pros know that 99.98 percent of an average audience won't notice a mistake unless the musicians themselves call attention to it.

Let's face it—you are going to make mistakes. It's part of the process. But if you let your mistakes get you all hot and bothered, your playing is going to become cramped and inhibited. If you simply relax, throw caution to the wind, and *allow* yourself the mistakes you will inevitably make, your playing will be freer, more playful, and more passionate. For now, you are only playing for yourself—are *you* going to be embarrassed by *your own* playing? Naahh!

Try This

1. A good way to get used to making mistakes is to force yourself to make *lots* of them. Try playing along with the tape while wearing a blindfold, or sitting in the dark.

This way, you'll have to rely solely on the feeling of the keyboard. Since you probably don't yet know the keyboard that well, you'll wind up making bargeloads of mistakes.

2. Try to play steadily no matter how badly you mess up, even if you can't seem to find *any* of the right notes. Be cool, be calm, don't stop the flow, have fun. After all, playing blindfolded is like playing pin the tail on the donkey—it's just a game. And since you're not competing with anyone, it's a game you can't lose.

Don't Think Too Much

■ Analytical thinking, an absolute necessity for fine-tuning an automobile engine or programming a computer, can serve us rather badly when it comes to music. When you plan ahead carefully and weigh every option, you run the danger of losing the ability to make free-flowing, spontaneous, creative sounds. Too much thinking often leads to trouble, especially for beginners.

The fact is, you shouldn't need to think much when playing along with the *Instant Piano* tape. The playing suggestions found throughout this book require a little extra *concentration* to execute, but not much *thought*. We've tried to do the thinking for you. You should clear your head, put on the tape, get the feel of the rhythm, and just let your fingers lead you.

Try This

1. To think less, pick only one thing to think about. Play along to a song on the tape and use only one note as your accompaniment. See how many things you can do with that one note.

2. Play your one note loudly, softly, slowly, quickly.

3. Hit your one note, stroke it, rest it, come back to it. Just think of that one note.

4. If you find your mind drifting, beginning to worry about what else you should be doing, just bring yourself back to your one note and concentrate on it again.

Don't Wrestle with the Gods and Expect to Win

■ Perhaps the most impossible demand of all is made when you begin comparing yourself to those who aren't your peers. If you are just starting to fool around with the piano, there's no point in moping about, wondering why you don't sound like Keith Jarrett. Whatever ability you have is a function of your training, education, and experience. If you didn't go to school with your household gods and you haven't trained with them over the years, you can't reasonably expect to wrestle with them and win.

Of course, we are motivated by the achievements of our idols. They show us what is possible to accomplish. We measure our own progress against theirs to see how far we have come, and how far we have yet to go. But to expect to measure up, to find ourselves the equals of our idols, is pure folly, and a common cause of much needless suffering, disappointment, and frustration.

1. Listen to one of your favorite records. Pick one that always causes your face to assume an expression of almost pained astonishment—sagging jaw, furrowed brow, bugged-out eyes, throbbing temples.

2. As you listen, try not to pay too much attention to the fusillade of notes whizzing by your head. Listen instead for the spirit, the emotion of the performance. Concentrate on *what* the performer is saying, not *how* your idol is saying it. Is the performance about love or lust? Despair or rapture? Boredom or hysteria? And how do you know? What is it in their performance that actually communicates the emotion?

3. When you think you've gotten the message, and you understand how it was transmitted, find the piece on the *Instant Piano* tape that most closely matches the feeling of the piece you were just listening to.

4. Play along using whatever expressive resources you now have to recreate the spiritual or emotional substance of your idol's performance. Don't think notes—think feeling. Try to use as few notes as you can to capture that feeling. You should find that, even without your idol's precision-tooled technical apparatus, you are able to evoke emotions and images with almost the same facility.

Play As If

The hardest thing about being a beginner is *sounding* like a beginner. Your fingers just don't do as they're told. Much of the time, you don't even know what to tell them to do. When you play, you stumble and fumble like a teenager attempting a first kiss. You're definitely not cool. And each blunder and misstep is just further confirmation of the embarrassing hopelessness of your case.

As a beginner—or even as a skilled musician learning a new technique or a new instrument—the severe judgments you pass on your own playing are unfair in at least two respects. First, as noted earlier, they result from the unreasonable demands you make on yourself. Second, and perhaps most significantly, you miss noting the real, honest strengths of the music you make. Your playing may not dazzle—no multidisc recording contract for you *now,* buddy—but it may yet be personal, sincere, and—dare we say it?—beautiful. It's important to recognize these qualities in your playing. If you don't, your enthusiasm for playing may wane rapidly.

Now if out of sheer cussed orneriness you *refuse* to hear these qualities in your music, try playing *as if* you did. Play *as if* you and your trusty piano are making the sweetest music this side of the heavenly choir. Play *as if* you know perfectly well what you are doing—play confidently, brashly, with unflappable self-assurance. Play as if you think your music is sublime, inventive, and magical, even (especially!) in its moment of starkest simplicity.

You might be surprised by the side effects of pretend self-assurance. You won't find yourself playing like Schnabel or Tatum, or even Jerry Lee Lewis; but you may begin to realize that the fundamental things that make *their* playing great are the same things that make *your* playing great—honest, emotional directness, wit, passion.

Try This

1. Play along with a selection on the tape.
2. *Love* your playing. Savor each ripe, luscious note. Admire the exquisitely piquant melding of your beguiling melodies with the taped accompaniment. Note the delicacy of your touch, your control, your sublime inventiveness, your limitless capacity for deep, rich, musical expression.
3. When the performance is over, buy yourself a drink, and leave yourself a big tip. Damn, you're good.

A Final Note

■ *Instant Piano* was created to help people have fun at the keyboard. If you ever find yourself falling into the "shoulds"—I should practice every day, I should work harder at this—go watch TV, put on the jogging suit and run your favorite path, read a racy mystery, or just sit and do nothing. Play the piano only when you feel like it. You'll still learn, and you'll keep coming back to it because it isn't a chore.

Chapter 3

You've Got Rhythm

Have you ever marched in a parade, or even just walked alongside one? You probably found that, without thinking about it for an instant, you wound up walking in step with the rhythm of the music. Or if you've ever discoed the night away under the flickering strobes and mirrored balls, chances are that you didn't need to be told how to move to the beat. The music set the groove and your feet did the rest.

Rhythm is second nature to us. We respond instinctively to it. We feel a beat and we dance, we clap our hands and snap our fingers, tap our toes and nod our heads. We can't help ourselves—it happens automatically.

Rhythm is often the element of a piece of music with which we identify most strongly. It's the heartbeat, the pulse of the music, the thing that presses it forward and makes it compelling. As a result, rhythm is possibly the single most important thing you should be aware of when you play. When you've got rhythm, you can't help but feel good and sound good.

How do you get rhythm? It's as easy as tapping your foot on the floor.

Getting into the Rhythm

■ "Down in the Disco," the first piece on Side 1 of the *Instant Piano* tape, has a driving beat. Listen and try to feel it with your whole body. Sway to it, dance to it, try to get hooked into the rhythm of the piece.

Try This

1. Put on the first song on Side 1. Listen to the drum at the beginning, before there is any music. The drum beats *tap, tap, tap, tap,* or "one, two, three, four." Let your foot tap the floor each time the drum taps. Keep your foot tapping at just that speed throughout the song. If you can do that, then you've got rhythm!

2. Each time your foot hits the floor, play a note. You can hit the same note repeatedly, or a different note each time. We're going to call each time your foot hits the floor one *beat* of the music. The diagram below shows that you are playing one note (N) for each beat (B):

N	N	N	N
B	B	B	B

Keep repeating this pattern of one note per beat all the way through the song.

3. Rewind the tape to the beginning and play the song again. This time, play *two* notes each time your foot hits the floor, that is, two notes per beat. Again you can play a

single note repeatedly, or you can keep moving between different notes. You'll probably like the sound you get when you vary the notes better than the sound of one repeated note—varied notes will sound more like a real melody or improvisation. The diagram below shows the new relationship of notes to beats:

```
|N   N  |N   N  |N   N  |N   N  |
|B      |B      |B      |B      |
```

4. Now try playing through the song using the pattern shown in the next diagram—one note for one beat followed by two notes played on the next beat:

```
|N      |N   N  |N      |N   N  |
|B      |B      |B      |B      |
```

Once again, you should try to vary the notes you play—but concentrate on sustaining the rhythmic pattern. Don't go so crazy choosing notes that the rhythm falters. The notes will come easily once you feel comfortable with the rhythm.

5. Make up some rhythm patterns of your own and play them with the same song. See how many different kinds of patterns you come up with. If you want, you might try patterns using three or four notes per beat. If you do, you'll probably want to simplify your choice of notes. Repeat notes if you must to keep the rhythm flowing. Remember, great music needn't be fiendishly difficult—just think of the success of songs like "One Note Samba." Keep it simple and enjoy yourself. You've got rhythm!

Resting or Leaving Space

■ So far, you've been playing one or more notes for every beat of music. You probably know from listening to music that professional musicians don't always play this way; they don't always "fill" each beat with notes. Instead they rest, or leave space, throughout their performance, just the way you pause to leave space between the words and sentences that you speak. Playing on every beat can make your music sound cramped, congested, and unrelaxed. When you rest, leaving space around the notes you play, you give your music an open, expansive, easygoing feeling.

Try This

1. Put on the second song on Side 1, "Uptown Hoedown." Tap out the rhythm of the piece with your foot.

2. Start by playing one note per beat, as you did before. Vary your notes, but keep repeating the rhythm pattern:

N	N	N	N
B	B	B	B

3. When you make it part of the way into the piece, start playing one note *every other beat*—one note as your foot hits the floor, then rest and play nothing the next time your foot hits the floor:

N		N	
B	B	B	B

21

Once again, you should try to vary the notes that you play, but focus on sustaining the rhythm pattern.

4. Try making up your own patterns of notes and rests. You can repeat each pattern for as long as you like, or you can switch off between two or more patterns. Or you can do both.

Now Forget Everything

■ When you improvise, you want to be able to cut loose and have a good time, to play freely and spontaneously. The last thing you want to do when you play is to tie your brain in knots thinking "note, rest, note, rest, note, note, rest . . . " Nothing could be more inhibiting. So after you've spent some time exploring, with some precision, the rhythm patterns presented in this chapter, the best thing you can do is—forget 'em! Don't even think of trying to memorize them—you don't need to. Instead, just try to play naturally, letting your instincts guide you. Play a little, rest a little, play . . . rest . . . play some more. If you think you have an interesting idea for a real rhythm pattern, by all means try it out. Just remember that you needn't play patterns. Play whatever comes to you *as you play*.

From time to time it does make sense to ask yourself a few questions like: "Am I playing with rhythm? Do I have a good mix of notes and rests? Am I playing too much?" If you find that you are dissatisfied with the rhythm, or rhythmic balance, of your playing, come back and work some more with the suggestions offered here. But when you're back on the track, stop thinking and just . . . PLAY!

Chapter 4
Piano ABC's

Great jazz pianists are expert scene painters and storytellers. Using sound, they tell us about what they are feeling or "seeing." A piano solo by Thelonious Monk can capture the desolate beauty of a city street at four in the morning. Oscar Peterson can tell the unhappy story of someone else's unhappy love affair. Chick Corea can sweep us away in the mad whirl of a fiesta or make us feel like children playing hopscotch in a schoolyard.

The Improviser's Story

■ When an improviser prepares to "sing" a story on the piano, he or she is confronted by the same sorts of questions a storyteller faces. The questions are about notes, though, not about words and how to speak them. The improviser asks: Which notes should I play, and in what order should I play them? Where on the keyboard should I play them—up high, down low, or somewhere in between? Which notes should I emphasize, and how can I emphasize them? When should I play loudly? Softly?

Should I play fast or slow? How should I play to recreate the sound of a mountain brook or to express the feeling I get walking alone on a beach on a warm, moonlit night?

Making Marvelous Melodies

■ As you play along with the tape, hunting for notes on the keyboard, you are making a *melody*. A melody is simply a sequence of notes. Melodies come in all shapes and sizes. The art of making them is one of music's greatest mysteries. Why are some melodies impossible to forget and others impossible to remember? No one really knows. The writing or improvising of a great melody is a kind of miracle: No one can explain how it happens or predict when and where it will happen.

Although no one can provide a surefire method for creating *great* melodies, we can give you some hints on how to make good melodies.

Make Your Melodies Move

Most good melodies *move*—they begin on one note, move up or down to another note, on to a third note, and so on and on. They may come to rest on a certain note here or there, or keep returning insistently to a particular note. Usually, though, a melody is in motion.

Black note by black note.

White note by white note.

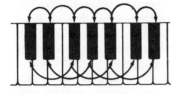

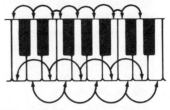

Skipping black notes.

Skipping white notes.

Try This

1. Begin without the tape. Pick a black note near the middle of the keyboard. Play as slowly as you have to to keep a steady beat. Move up the keyboard note by note on the black keys. When you've played several black notes, come back down the same way you went up: slowly, steadily. As you play, keep each note depressed until you are ready to move on to the next one. This will give you a smooth, continuous sound. There. You've just made a simple melody.

2. Now try skipping certain black notes. Pick a black note to the left of center on the keyboard. Keeping a slow steady beat, move up through the black notes skipping *every other one*. Play several notes going up and then come down the same way. Try it again skipping two black notes, or three black notes, as many as you want.

3. Now play a single melody by going from black note to black note as well as skipping certain black notes. You might move up the keyboard note by note and come back down by skips of three, four, or more black notes. You can use a combination of the two. Ask yourself what kinds of images or feelings your melody suggests. What kind of story does it tell? Use your feelings and any stories inside you to shape the melody. Don't worry about making mistakes—you can't possibly make any!

4. *Now* you can put on the tape. Start with one of the slower selections. Tap your foot to keep the beat. Play a melody on the black notes along with the tape. Keep it simple—just move up and down the keyboard note by note or by skips, or some combination of the two. Remember that there is no *right* way to play. The only way that matters is the way that pleases you. Just try to express what you feel, be it lethargy, anxiety, sadness, joy, anger, annoyance, peace, or love.

Drawing a Melody Line

If you saw the notes of your melody as points on a graph, the line that connects them would show you your melody line and the shape of it. For example, look at the melody in illustration (a) below. It begins on one note that is played four times, makes a large skip of three black notes, and then comes back down in small skips to the original note.

Another example of drawing a melody line is shown in illustration (b). It starts on one note, moves down a note, down another note, rises one note, goes down one note, then skips right up to the original note.

(a)

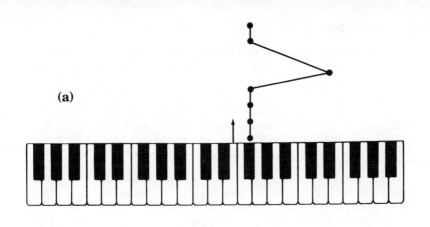

(b)

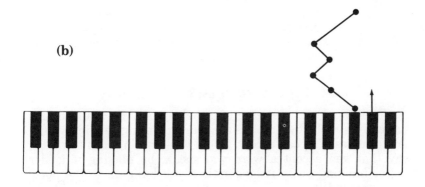

27

Melody Patterns

Composers usually repeat melody lines, or shapes, within one song. Thus the melody shape in illustration (a) might be played a few times, then the melody in illustration (b) a few times, or the shapes might be mixed and repeated. You can be sure, though, if a composer has a good melody line, he or she will come back to it over and over in any one piece.

Try This

Try playing along with some of the selections on the tape. A good way to begin would be by trying to match the mood of a particular piece on the tape with the feeling of a shape you draw or imagine. Think of big sweeping shapes, or sharp zigzag shapes made of many turns. Try to make the shape of your melody reflect what you are feeling. Listen to an accompaniment track to see what sort of melody shape it might "want," and draw a new shape to suit it. Whatever you do, continue to play steadily and rhythmically, but stay related. If this means playing very slowly and simply, that's okay. You're trying to develop a feeling for creating melody shapes, not rehearsing for your Carnegie Hall debut. So . . . take it easy and have fun.

The Right Emphasis—Accenting

■ The sound and meaning of a melody may be changed dramatically simply by emphasizing, or accenting, an individual note or notes. You can accent a note you play in much the same way that you accent a word you speak, by playing it louder and/or hanging on to it longer than you hang on to the notes that surround it.

1. Rest the five fingers of one hand on five adjacent keys on the piano (black or white). Play up and down using the following finger pattern: right hand 1-2-3-4-5-4-3-2-1, or left hand 5-4-3-2-1-2-3-4-5. The thumb is 1 and the pinky is 5. Play through the pattern several times. Then, as you continue to play, begin to emphasize the note played by your thumb by striking it harder than the other notes. To be heard as an accented note, this note must be louder than the others in the pattern:

1-2-3-4-5-4-3-2-**1**-2-3-4-5-4-3-2-**1**

After a few repetitions of this pattern, shift the accent to the note played by your second finger. Then try accenting with your third finger, then your fourth, and your fifth. Try patterns in which every other note is accented. Invent your own patterns to accent and play.

2. Put on one of the slower selections from the tape and play along. As you play, try out different patterns of accent: every fourth note, every other note, and so on.

3. Play along with another selection from the tape. Forget about the fixed patterns of accents. Just relax, play playfully, and let the accents fall where they may. You've now got another trick up your sleeve; if you are like most musicians, you won't hesitate to use it.

Stroking, Hitting, and Using the Pedal

■ Gently stroking notes will give you soft, dreamy sounds, while hitting notes will give you loud, boisterous sounds. These two techniques and one more can be used to achieve other interesting effects as well.

Choppy

A single melodic line can convey very different messages or emotions depending upon how it is played—smoothly, slickly, gracefully, or choppily, disconnectedly, abruptly. To get a staccato machine-gun style, here are a few hints.

Try This

1. It's easy to get a choppy, disconnected sound on the piano. You can do it simply by playing with only one finger. When you play this way, the finger must come up off the note you've just played before you can play any other notes. This means that there will always be a space—even if it's only a very short one—between the notes. The *amount* of space between the notes you play determines how choppy your playing will be.

2. Play along with selections from the tape in this choppy, discontinuous style. Listen carefully to the relationship between your playing and the music on the tape. What sort of overall sound do you get when you play choppily against a smooth, glassy, musical background?

Against a punchy, rockin' background? Which sort of combination do you like better?

Smooth

The fundamental principle of seamless playing is obvious enough—avoid leaving silent spaces between notes. If you do so, your melody will flow in a continuous stream of sound. But how to do it?

Again, the idea is simple. When moving from one note to the next, make sure you hold the first down until the second begins to sound. Just as the second sounds, release the first. The first note will flow imperceptibly into the second, without interruption, and without the two blurring together.

Try This

1. When you feel that you can gently unfurl a streaming ribbon of melody using two fingers, try playing along with the tape. Keep your playing simple and rhythmic. Concentrate on the *quality* of the sound you are producing—don't worry too much about the notes.

2. You can also make singing, fluid melodies using more than two fingers on one hand. The trick, again, is to lift off of a struck key just as you strike the new key. Place your thumb and your next two fingers on three adjacent keys. Strike with your thumb and hold on to the note. Then, just as you strike the next key with your index finger, lift up with your thumb. Go on to the third key and come back down. Maintain a moderate, even volume.

3. Try this again using four fingers, and then five.

4. Play along with a selection from the tape. Use your newfound techniques to make slinky, mellifluous melodies, playing with two to five fingers. Listen for the way in which your melody interacts qualitatively with the musical background.

Pedal

There is another way to achieve smooth sounds on your keyboard, notes that seem to go on forever, floating, hovering in the air. To produce this haunting effect, you can use the right foot pedal on your piano. This device holds the sound of a note for as long as you keep your foot down.

Try This

1. Play a note without using the pedal. Then press down the right foot pedal and play the same note. Listen to it. Can you hear the difference?

2. Push down the pedal, play a note, then another note. Listen as both notes are held in the air. Then do the same thing, but lift your foot off the pedal while your finger is still holding down the second note. Do you hear the difference?

3. Experiment pressing down and releasing the pedal as you play notes. Get used to the feeling and sound of blending notes into one another, of holding them, releasing them, cutting them short.

4. When you think you have a good sense of the pedal, play along with the tape using these devices. It will probably be easier at first if you play along to a slow song. The pedal's lingering notes often work well with slow, lilting melodies. Try not to keep your foot down all the time though—the pedal is for special effect, to wring the most out of certain notes, to hold the last notes in melody lines, to make smooth transitions from some notes to others, to hold a long note while you play others over it. If you use it *all* the time, however, your playing becomes "muddy," with no distinciton between any notes.

Potpourri

■ There are many more techniques you can use singly or together to make your playing more interesting. A few of them are listed below.

- Play at different speeds. Play fast, slow, in between. Try all three within one piece.
- Vary the volume of your playing. Play loudly, softly, at a whisper, at a roar. Again, use changes in volume within one song.
- Utilize the entire keyboard. Play up, down, and all around to get different effects.
- Combine the techniques you have learned about so far. One by one, start to use all the devices you know of within each song.

Don't Throw Your Hands Up

■   If you had to think about each little thing you have read, at each moment you are playing, no one would blame you if you screamed and walked away from the keyboard forever. Don't despair. The skills that you are reading about become second nature very quickly. You will find yourself doing things automatically without ever giving them a second thought. When you feel like thinking, choose one or two effects to concentrate on, and forget about the rest. When you don't feel like utilizing the gray cells, forget about *everything*. Sooner or later, it will all show up in your playing.

Chapter 5
Tricks of the Trade

The difference between doing something well and *really* well is often not very great. A few dabs of paint on a canvas can change a skillful but uninspired work into a lively, sparkling painting. In this chapter, we will help you put some "finishing touches" on your *Instant Piano* performance. We'll show you some special "tricks" you can use with the individual pieces on Side 1. Equipped with these tricks of the piano trade, you'll be able to add more excitement and make each piece you play unique.

"Down in the Disco" (Side 1, Piece 1)

The first piece on Side 1 is "Down in the Disco," the kind of piece a record company exec might call an MOR piece. *MOR* is record-industry jargon for "middle-of-the-road." An MOR record usually has too strong a rock beat for playing in dentists' offices and elevators, but too weak a rock beat to make it with the Black Sabbath/Van Halen crowd. People like Carly Simon, Linda Ronstadt, and James Taylor are considered MOR artists.

Their music appeals to the great "middle-of-the-listening public." One good way to get a strong, punchy sound when you improvise to "Down in the Disco" is to use deep, powerful bass notes. Here's how to do it.

Try This

   1. Listen carefully to "Down in the Disco" without actually playing along. Notice that, once you get past a short introduction, the piece has two distinct sections, and these sections repeat alternately. The first section has a fairly bright, cheery sound. The second section begins with a rapid flurry of notes played on a harplike instrument. Then the sound of the piece gets a bit "darker."
   2. The characteristic sound of each of the two sections of "Down in the Disco" is determined by the bass notes that undergird them. The first section is anchored by this bass note:

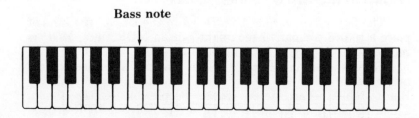

Bass note

The second section's principal bass note is:

Bass note

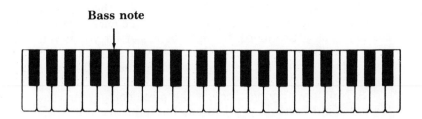

When you play along with this piece, you can increase its forward thrust by reinforcing these bass notes, pounding them out yourself in the appropriate spots.

Try playing along with the piece using only bass notes, matching the notes shown above to their respective sections. Use one of the rhythm patterns given here, or make up some of your own:

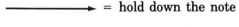

$\longrightarrow$ = hold down the note

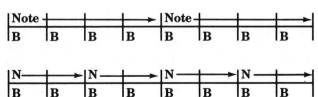

Take care to shift back and forth between the two bass notes at the right time. Use your ear and the cues given in the music as your guides. It might be easier for you if you keep your fingers resting on the notes you expect to play even when you're not actually playing them. This will make them much easier to find.

3. Now try playing through the piece doing your customary right-hand improvisation, but punctuate it with booming left-hand bass notes. Keep track of the sections as they fly by, making sure you are putting the bass notes in the right place. You'll soon hear the difference and not have to think about it. Let yourself be guided by your ear and the cues provided by the music on the tape. See if you can make the piece rock a little bit harder than it already does by really punching out those bass notes. Keep things *very* simple. Use only the simplest rhythm patterns for the bass and keep your right-hand melodies clean and lean. You can do it! Just take it nice and slow.

"Uptown Hoedown" (Side 1, Piece 2)

The second piece on Side 1 is a typical country song. Country music is simple music with clean, uncomplicated sounds and strong melodies. Here are a few suggestions for playing along to "Uptown Hoedown."

38

Try This

1. A common rhythm used in country music is to play two notes for each beat. Put on "Uptown Hoedown" and jump around the right-hand side of the keyboard using this rhythm pattern:

N N	N N	N N	N N	
B	B	B	B	Repeat

2. Certain notes are used often in country music. With your left hand, hold down the note shown. With your right hand alternate playing any of the other three notes shown. As the sound of the bass note your left hand plays begins to fade, hit it again and hold it down, continuing to play the three higher notes.

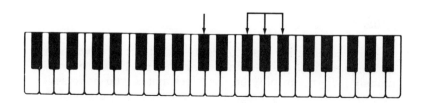

3. Now try reversing the above notes. Play the single note with your right hand, on the right half of the keyboard. Alternate the other three notes with your left hand. Get into that square-dance mood and bounce, hop, and roll.

"Summer Mornings with You" (Side 1, Piece 3)

The third piece on Side 1, like the first piece, also has an MOR-ish sound to it. This piece, however, is a ballad. When you play along with a bittersweet, mellow, romantic piece like "Summer Mornings," try to capture a dreamy, almost wistful feeling. Here are a few suggestions for doing just that.

Try This

1. One effective way to create sweetness and warmth on the piano is to play two notes *together* that blend harmoniously. When you play on the black notes, you have several of these sweetly harmonious pairs at your disposal:

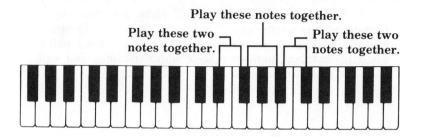

Play these two notes together.

Play these notes together.

Play these two notes together.

Play each of these pairs a few times. To begin with, play them on the right-hand side of the piano. Play using either one finger on each hand or two fingers on one hand, whichever feels most comfortable.

2. Now put on "Summer Mornings." As an experiment, try playing through the entire piece using nothing but these three pairs of notes.

3. When you're done, rewind to the beginning of "Summer Mornings." Play through the piece again using the techniques explored in the two preceding chapters. As you improvise, look for opportunities to add two-note pairs.

4. As an additional experiment, try playing these two-note pairs in other regions of the keyboard. Notice how shifting the region in which a pair is played can change its color. What do these pairs sound like played way down low, and way up high? Can you use these contrasts expressively or dramatically while playing with "Summer Mornings"?

5. SPECIAL ADDED BONUS! Here are three more harmonious two-note pairs you can use with "Summer Mornings." Repeat the exercises above using these pairs. Then try mixing them into your improvisation. You will have *six* pairs to choose from when you play!

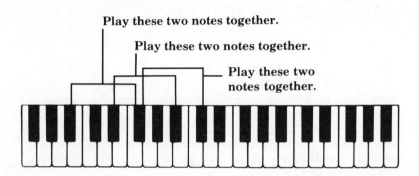

Play these two notes together.

Play these two notes together.

Play these two notes together.

"Breakin' Out" (Side 1, Piece 4)

"Uptown Hoedown" took you dancing in the country, now "Breakin' Out" will take you dancing in the heart of the city. "Breakin' Out" has the sounds of robots and computers. It was designed for breakdancing. It's got the funky, twisted rhythm, outer-space drum sounds, and manic energy that the kids with the untied high-top athletic shoes and hooded nylon running jackets crave.

1. The key to playing successfully with a piece like "Breakin' Out" is to keep your part simple, repetitive, and rhythmically right on the money. It's more important that the notes you play be crisp and accurately placed than it is for them to trace out some inspired melody. Melody itself doesn't count for much in music like this—rhythm is all. In a piece like "Breakin' Out," most of the excitement comes from the rhythmic momentum and complexity created by superimposing layers of simple but interlocked rhythm patterns. You can add to that excitement by playing patterns of your own. Here are two possibilities:

a.

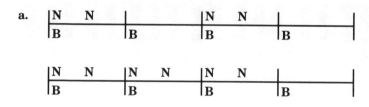

b.

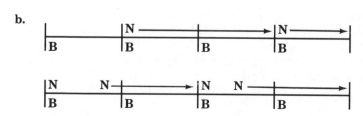

When you play these patterns, or patterns of your own, keep in mind that you don't really need to change notes all that often. You can hang on to one note for a long time, playing it through multiple repetitions of a single rhythmic pattern, and still get a hot sound. Or, you can work a series of rhythmic variations on that same note, taking it through a number of *different* patterns. Whatever you do, keep the melody spare and simple, and focus on the rhythm.

2. Here's a way to intensify the sound of those repeated, rhythmic notes. Let's say you're wailing on this note:

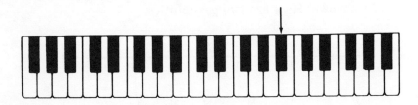

If you count up or down five black notes from that note, you will find notes that are "identical" in sound to your original note. True, these notes will be *pitched* higher or lower than your starting note, but if you play one (or both) of these notes together with the original note, they will blend so perfectly you probably won't be able to tell them apart.

Same notes

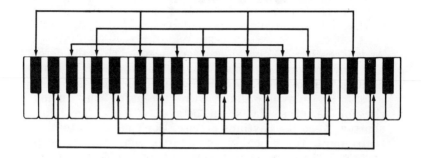

Any two black notes five black notes apart will exhibit this property. Pairs of notes possessing this property are called *octaves;* playing the two notes together is called *playing in octaves*.

Let's go back to that rhythm pattern you were playing. You can greatly intensify the sound you get when playing that pattern by playing it in octaves. Play the pattern on one note, using your right hand, and at the same time play the same pattern on the note five notes away, using your left. In other words, play the pattern on, for example, these two notes simultaneously:

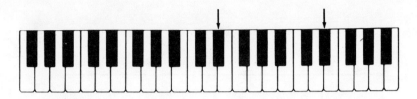

As you continue to play the pattern, you can shift the notes you play in *parallel octaves*. If you move your right hand note up a note, move its octave companion likewise.

3. Try playing along with "Breakin' Out" using rhythm patterns played in octaves. Attack the notes sharply. Keep the rhythms precise. Don't be afraid to play really hard. You probably won't break your piano. And if you stay off your head, you won't break anything else, either.

"Blues in an Instant" (Side 1, Piece 5)

Let's say you're all broke down 'cause your baby done gone and left you all alone. You've got the blues. Let's say you haven't got a dime, nothing more than the rags on your back, and you've got nowhere to go. You've got the blues. Let's say that hard luck and trouble have been your only friends, and you've been down ever since you were ten. Lord knows you've got the blues.

Over the years, musicians have developed a special musical form, using a fixed and repeated sequence of harmonies, designed specifically for music that expresses these feelings. "Blues in an Instant" is a typical blues number. It is the sort of blues a jazz group would have played in the early 1950s, particularly if the group had been led by someone like Miles Davis or Red Garland or Wynton Kelly.

Try This

1. The blues, in addition to being a music form, are closely identified with a series of notes. On the black keys, these notes are *all* the black notes and one white note.

Practice playing up and down the black notes adding the new white note to get the sound of the blues notes in your ears and the feel of them under your fingers. Also try playing in different regions of the keyboard.

2. When you are comfortable with the blues sound, use it to play along with "Blues in an Instant." At first, the music you are making might seem a little dissonant. The quality of sound that you might be objecting to, however, is precisely the sound *of* the blues. Remember, the blues are usually about sorrow, hardship, and pain. What better way to express these feelings than with sounds that are raw, gritty, and slightly unpleasant?

3. Remember playing pairs of notes with "Summer Mornings"? You can also use pairs of notes with "Blues in an Instant." In fact, because of the deliberate *dirtiness* of the sound that is characteristic of the blues, you can play almost *any* pair of black notes with "Blues in an Instant." Any combination you devise will probably have a bracingly bitter, gutsy, bluesy sound. Here are a few of the more savory pairs.

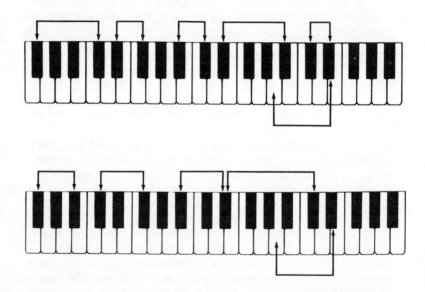

You can do almost anything you want with these pairs— make a whole piece out of them, hammer away at them until your fingertips are bruised and calloused (you gotta pay your dues if you wanna play the blues), or use them intermittently to spice up your single-note playing.

"Pushy" (Side 1, Piece 6)

For the last piece on Side 1, it's time once again to put on your dancin' shoes and prepare to strut your stuff. "Pushy" is the distilled essence of modern American dance music—fast, urgent, a little pushy. It's music that wants to *make* you dance— or make you play along, or maybe do both.

If you decide to play now and dance later, here are a few pointers for "Pushy."

Try This

1. "Pushy" is one of those pieces, like "Breakin' Out," where melodically, less is more. The piece is so strong and so complex rhythmically that a busy, jumpy melody would be at best superfluous and at worst distracting. As with "Breakin' Out," your playing on "Pushy" will be most effective when it is spare, rhythmic, and precise.

One trick you might apply to "Pushy" is this: Play the piano as though you were playing a drum—a tuned drum. Use either two fingers on one hand, or one finger on each hand, as if they were drumsticks, and drum away at the black keys percussively.

For example, try playing on these two notes, striking the lower of the two with the index finger of your left hand and the other with the index finger of your right hand.

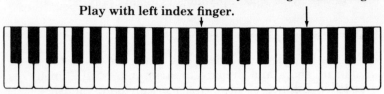

Play with left index finger. Play with right index finger.

You will notice (we hope) that these two notes, being five black notes apart, are *octaves*. You should "drum" on these two notes using a rhythm pattern like this (notice the alternation of hands):

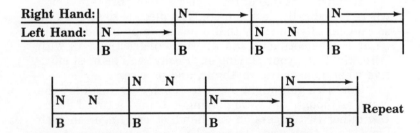

Once you get the hang of "drumming" like this, you can move your octaves around—up and down—on the keyboard in parallel moves creating simple melodic shapes out of shifting octaves.

50

2. If you want to "drum" with two fingers on one hand, you should pick pairs of notes that are close together. Here are a few pairs to experiment with:

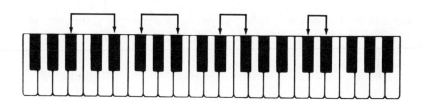

You can investigate other pairs on your own.

When you drum using these pairs, the principle is the same as when you used fingers on separate hands. You employ exactly the same sorts of rhythm patterns, but execute them using fingers on one hand. Whenever possible, drum with your thumb and your first two fingers. They are much stronger than the last two fingers on your hand, and so make much sturdier and more reliable drumsticks.

3. Turn on "Pushy." Drum your way through the piece. Keep your attack sharp and accurate. Imagine yourself to actually *be* the drummer. You are responsible for keeping the rhythm rock steady, but also for pushing the song forward. Push hard, but don't lose the pulse.

A Full Bag of Tricks

■ Now you're familiar with many tricks musicians use to put that polish and finish on their playing. But there are more! The best way to find them is just to play and feel free to do new and different things whenever you want. Sometimes you'll fall flat on your musical derrière; but occasionally, you'll rise to the heights and discover a new and exciting device of your own. It won't be long before you have a full bag of tricks to make your playing sparkle.

Now, on to the white notes!

Chapter 6
White on White

Just as good mountain climbers know where they can stomp and where they should use caution, wise piano players know the "steady rocks" and "wobbly stones" of the keyboard. As you move on to playing with the white keys in this chapter, you'll learn to distinguish between the two.

The Way of the White Notes

■ Physically, most people find it easier to play on the white notes than on the black. The white keys are both longer and broader than the black keys, which are skinny and short. It's easier for your fingers to find the bigger white keys and, when they do, they tend to stay put. Were there times your fingers simply missed the black keys they'd been so carefully aimed at? And were there other times when, after you'd found the black notes your fingers sought, they simply fell off, like inebriated buffoons in a high-wire act? When you play on the white notes, these sorts of silly mishaps occur rarely, if ever.

When you do play on the white notes, though, you face a new challenge. As you play along with some selections on the tape, you'll find that all the white notes are good, sturdy stepping stones across the brook. On others, you'll notice that some of the white notes work better than others while one or two may sound a bit wobbly, or a bit "off."

There are two white notes than can ruffle your musical feathers. As you can see, they are the same two notes up and down the keyboard.

←Etc.   Etc.→

What to do about these pesky critters? As some people skip over slippery stones in a brook rather than tread on them lightly, your best bet might be to avoid these notes at first if you find they get in the way during certain songs.

Try This

1. To begin, you may want to mark the notes to avoid with small pieces of masking tape.
2. Play up and down through the notes that remain. The sound of this series of notes should remind you of the sound you get playing up and down through the black notes. The notes have the same relationship to each other.

3. Turn back to Chapter 4 and try some of the exercises there, this time playing them on the white notes. Keep in mind that everything you did on the black notes can be done on the white notes—and it should be easier. The only thing that has changed is the color of the keys.

4. Now, start playing through the selections on Side 2 of the *Instant Piano* tape. When you hear that notes are "clunking," leave out the two offending notes marked with masking tape on your piano. Make use of all the parameters you explored in Chapter 4—volume, tempo, attack, and so on—to create scintillating and soulful melodies. As you've already learned to do when you start something new, keep things simple. Playing on the white notes can be a breeze. Take your time, don't push, and have a ball!

Return of the Exiles

The two notes that got packed off to musical Siberia for several selections don't have to be kept in exile forever. They're not bad or wicked notes. You simply have to know how to handle them to make them behave, and then you can use them in all the songs you play along with. You'll have more notes to choose from as you play—always a benefit—and these notes may give unusual color to your music.

1. *Don't give the exiles undue emphasis.* Like the unsteady rocks in the stream, don't stomp on the exile notes incessantly. Avoid beginning and ending your melodies, or small sections of your melodies, on them. Avoid playing them on strong beats—keep them weak and they won't be inclined to rebel.

2. *Use these notes in passing.* Figuratively, this means to use the exiles sparingly, intermittently. Literally, this means to use them to pass *between* the notes that surround them. For example, take the note shown here:

One good way to use it would be as passage between its two adjacent white notes:

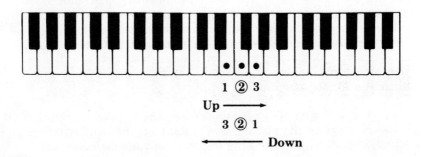

1 ② 3

Up ⟶

3 ② 1

⟵ Down

You can use the other exile the same way. They sound best when preceded or followed by an adjacent note.

3. *Observe the strong directional tendency of these notes.* Huh? The notes in question have what musicians call *directional tendencies.* This means that when you play one of them, your ear will probably be most satisfied and pleased if you move in a definite direction immediately afterward. Specifically, one of these notes wants to move down to the white note directly adjacent to it, as shown:

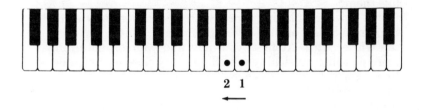

The other note wants to move up to its next-door neighbor:

1. Without the tape, spend some time making unaccompanied melodies that use all of the white notes. Make use of the three guidelines given above. Keep in mind that they are *only* guidelines, and not commandments. Indeed, you should try to play in ways that deliberately flout any guidelines, keeping an ear open for unusual and compelling sounds. Rules are made to be broken—and some of the most desirable outcomes are precisely the results of ignoring them.

2. Now try playing along with a selection, any selection, from Side 2 of the *Instant Piano* tape. Play using all of the white notes. At first, you may find yourself obtaining more pleasing musical results if you stay close to the guidelines. You'll have to discover for yourself the best uses for the new and potentially troublesome notes now at your disposal. If you play a lot and use your ears, you should find that *all* of the white notes can be used on *all* of the selections on the second side of the tape. Happy hunting!

"Switch!"

■ The last song on Side 2 (Piece 7) of the *Instant Piano* tape is called "Switch!" If you have already listened to this selection, it's obvious why the piece is so named—regularly, throughout the song, the whole band whistles and then shouts: "Switch!"

Believe it or not, the purpose of these intermittent exclamations is not to get you to change the brand of cigarettes you smoke or the kind of antiperspirant you use. Instead, you are actually being given playing instructions. Here's how it works:

Begin the tune by playing on the white notes alone. You can use either the whole lot of them, or the group that was picked out at the beginning of the chapter. When the band shouts "Switch!" immediately begin playing on the *black notes* only. Then, at the next "Switch!" shift your playing back to the white notes as you are cued by the band. Make sure you start playing on the white notes or you will have reversed the alternating pattern of white and black. However, even if you start off on the wrong set of keys, you'll soon begin to hear and feel which group of notes to use.

Play Now, Read Later

■ You've read this chapter. Now put the book down, turn on the tape, and play through each of the white-note selections on Side 2. Forget about the instructions you've been given. Have some fun on your own, exploring the brave new world of the white notes. Let yourself be bold, frivolous, daft, and intense. Listen for the different types of sound you can get using all of the white keys. Compare those sounds with the sounds you get from the black keys. Explore the differences and exploit them. Be easy on yourself. Be patient. Play, listen, and learn. It's just beautiful music—and you're the one who's making it. When you're ready, come on back to the book and try some of the ideas in the next chapter.

Chapter 7
More Tricks

In Chapter 5, you learned several techniques to apply to the individual songs on Side 1 of the *Instant Piano* tape. In this chapter, it's time to expand your bag of tricks and apply some simple but great-sounding devices to each piece on Side 2 of the tape.

"Jump Rock" (Side 2, Piece 1)

"Jump Rock" is, as the name suggests, another jumpin' *Instant Piano* rocker. Like all of the other rock tunes on the tape, it has two distinct sections. Here, though, there's a twist in the old rock formula: the second section is slower than the first section. In fact, the second section is *exactly* half the speed of the first section—it's in what musicians call "half-time." This is something you should be able to capitalize on as you improvise.

Try This

1. The preceding chapter suggested you get started playing on the white notes by marking and avoiding the two notes likely to cause you grief:

When you play with "Jump Rock," avoid the marked notes during the fast sections of the song, but make full use of them during the slow sections. This will help you to distinguish *melodically* between the two sections of the piece and will help keep you out of trouble during the fast sections. (You may find that you can really lay into the marked notes on the slow sections, provided you take note of their directional tendencies, explained in the preceding chapter.)

2. You can also use melodic rhythms to heighten the contrast between the two repeated sections of "Jump Rock." For example, try using fixed rhythm patterns when playing on the fast section, keeping the melody itself simple and spare. Here are a few of the many possible patterns:

a.

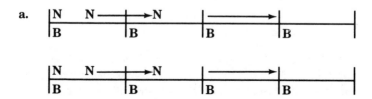

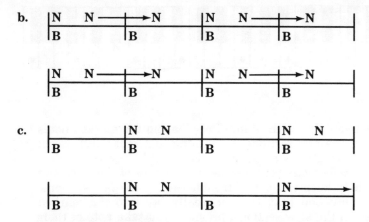

b.

c.

Then, when you play on the slow section, you can make your melodies more free-flowing, less rhythmically confined. When the fast section begins again, you can dig in with a rockin' rhythm. The rhythmic contrast between the two sections will give your playing a great sound.

"Canon in C, à la Pachelbel" (Side 2, Piece 2)

"Pachelbel's Canon" is a piece of classical music that continues to grow in popularity. The piece, written in the last half of the seventeenth century by the Baroque composer Johannes Pachelbel, seems to turn up everywhere: at weddings, as part of the soundtrack of movies such as *Ordinary People*, in music boxes and jewelry cases, and on the records of avant-garde rock musicians like Brian Eno. The piece was originally written for performance by a string ensemble. Here, we've adapted it for the keyboard.

Try This

1. One way to get started playing on "Pachelbel's Canon" is by playing straight down through the white notes. The illustrations below show you four possible sequences of notes. Observe that the first three sequences, though including all of the white notes, each start on a different note.

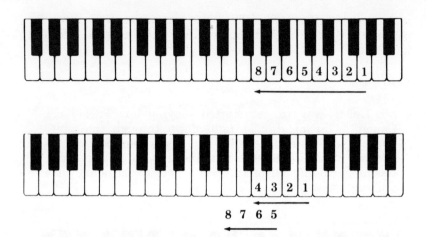

At the beginning of the piece, play the first or last sequence repeating it several times and holding each note for two beats. Then, play through sequence 2 and then sequence 3. Hold each note for two beats and try not to skip beats when moving between sequences. You can also try to play one or more sequences hitting one note for *each* beat, not every other beat.

2. Experiment with other continuous sequences of notes. In particular, you might try playing *up* through the sequences, that is, start on the low note of the sequence and play up toward the high note, once again holding each note for two beats and skipping to a new sequence when you hit the top.

3. Try experimenting with the pedal (the sustain pedal) when you play to "Pachelbel's Canon." Here, you can use the pedal to get a diffuse, dreamy sound. Improvise slowly on the white notes while keeping the sustain pedal depressed. Let the notes blur together to create a smoky haze of sound. Lift up on the pedal whenever the sound gets too murky. Play the music you expect to hear when you get to heaven.

"Fifties Rock" (Side 2, Piece 3)

What do you think of when you think of the 1950s? Ike? Bobby sox, saddle shoes, ponytails, and Annette Funicello? Cars with fins? Songs with lyrics like "Doo-wop, doo doo-doo wop"? "Fifties Rock" is one-hundred percent early rock 'n' roll—simple sounds and a steady beat. Here's how to play it.

Try This

Listen carefully to the rhythm of "Fifties Rock." The song uses a rocking, three-notes-to-the-beat rhythm. Listen to the piano on this piece. It chugs along like this:

N N N	N N N	N N N	N N N
B	B	B	B

You can also use these variations. (R) equals Rest.

N ——→	N ——→N	N ——→	N ——→N	Repeat
B	B	B	B	

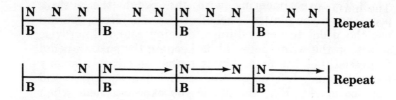

"'Lectronic Lady'" (Side 2, Piece 4)

"'Lectronic Lady" is an example of a subgenre of contemporary rock music called *synth-rock*. The music takes its name from the electronic sound musicians get from their synthesizers—rich and exotic tones and textures. As played by groups with names like Joy Division, New Order, and Orchestral Manoeuvres in the Dark, synth-rock represents the union of Eighties microchip computer technology with the pulsating rhythms of rock 'n' roll.

Try This

1. The dark, brooding sound of "'Lectronic Lady" derives in part from the piece's bass line and the chords that rest on it. The bass line relies heavily on this note.

The harmony of the piece is based largely on these three notes. It changes only for the short section in the middle.

Play these notes together.

You should use this bass note and these harmony notes as the touchstones of your improvisation. If you hover on or about them, you'll find it easier to match the piece's moody ambience.

2. To get your improvised melodies even closer to the spirit of "'Lectronic Lady," you might use these eight notes when playing the section in the middle of the song.

Notice that the top and bottom notes are the same as the bass note.

3. You'll also find that a number of two-note combinations sound good with "'Lectronic Lady." Try these, and then come up with some of your own.

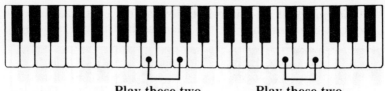

Play these two
notes together.

Play these two
notes together.

Play these two
notes together.

Play these two
notes together.

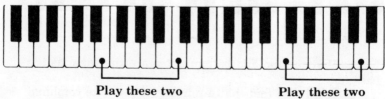

Play these two
notes together.

Play these two
notes together.

68

"Honky-Tonk Blues" (Side 2, Piece 5)

"Honky-Tonk Blues" is what's known as boogie-woogie blues—boogie-woogie being a style of piano playing characterized by chugging, trainlike, left-hand bass lines and blues-drenched right-hand leads. The form of "Honky-Tonk Blues" is very similar to that of "Blues in an Instant" on Side 1, but the feeling here is more raw, more "down-and-dirty."

Try This

1. Being a blues, "Honky-Tonk Blues" should be played using the blues notes. The notes you want are shown here:

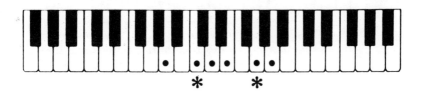

The lone black note and the two white notes marked with stars are the bluesiest notes of all. When you play, you may want to lean hard on them—they'll give you the dirty, abrasive sound associated with boogie-woogie blues.

2. Make the most of boogie-woogie rhythm. You can do this by flailing away at any of the two-note combinations shown below.

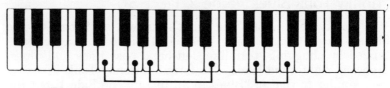

Play these two notes together.   Play these two notes together.   Play these two notes together.

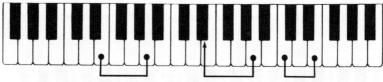

Play these two notes together.   Play these two notes together.   Play these two notes together.

3. There is a section in the last half of this piece in which all the music seems to start and stop spasmodically. Don't worry—there's nothing wrong with your tape. We've thrown in a little musical device known as "stop time" (which was also used in "Blues in an Instant" on Side 1). During stop time, the rhythm of the piece seems to stop, only to start again a few beats later. You may hear that whenever the music starts up, it always does so right on the beat. So in fact, the rhythm of the piece is never really lost—just not heard.

During a stop-time interlude, the soloist—you—is supposed to take center stage and wail with all he or she has got.

"Just Before Dawn" (Side 2, Piece 6)

The next song is one you're likely to hear at quarter to three on a Saturday morning if you stop into a local jazz club. It's dreamy, lazy, late-night jazz.

Try This

1. "Just Before Dawn" is a white-note piece. When you play on it, try to use all of the white notes. But to give your performance the smoky sound of late-night jazz, there are a few black notes you might want to toss in from time to time.

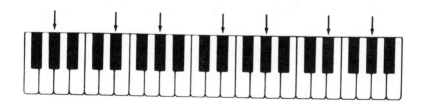

Use these black notes as *passing tones*—that is, pass through them while traveling from one adjacent white note to another.

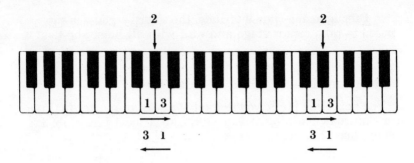

There are two typical jazz "licks" you can play that make use of these two black notes. Use the black notes as "approach" notes to their adjacent white notes.

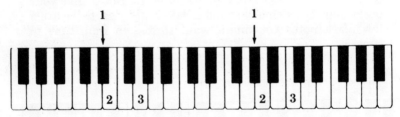

You can play these three-note patterns over and over again. Try using the three-to-one rhythm pattern you explored in "Fifties Rock," earlier on Side 2.

N	N	N	N	N	N	N	N	N	N	N	N	Repeat
B			B			B			B			

2. "Just Before Dawn" is also a good piece to play with lots of sustain pedal. You might try playing very few notes, spaced very far apart, with the sustain pedal depressed. Try to get a hazy, three-in-the-morning sound.

"Switch!" (Side 2, Piece 7)

If you can't get to the Carnaval in Rio this year, "Switch!" is the next best thing to being there. It has the percolating percussion sounds and infectious rhythms of Latin music—the music of the bossa nova, the samba, the tango, the merengue—as well as the driving beat of today's rock 'n' roll.

If you've already listened to "Switch!" you should have no trouble knowing how the song got its name. At regular intervals the band whistles and shouts out "Switch!" As was mentioned in the last chapter, this is your cue to switch from playing on the white notes to playing on the black notes or vice versa. Here are a few more ideas to enhance your playing on "Switch!"

Try This

1. Begin playing "Switch!" on the white notes. The first time the band whistles and shouts "Switch!" start playing on the black notes. The next time the band shouts "Switch!" start playing on the white notes . . . and so on through the piece. It's important that you keep track of where you are in the tune at any given point. However, after playing through it once or twice, you'll start to have a natural feel and ear for when to make the changes. You won't have to keep track at all then. If you get lost, and you can't use your ear to figure out where you are, your best bet is to return to the beginning of the tune.

2. The bass line for "Switch!" is really very simple—simple enough for you to play along with. During the white-note section of the piece, the bass line moves back and forth between these two notes (you'll hear a few extra notes thrown in on the tape, but these aren't really essential).

The bass line starts on the higher of the two notes (1), and then alternates with the second note using this rhythm.

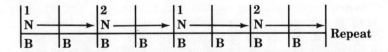

During the black-note section of the piece, the bass line alternates between these two notes:

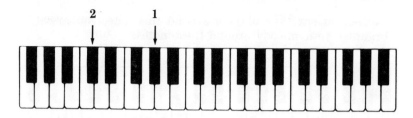

They are played using the same pattern of rhythmic alternation used in the white-note section.

Try to play along with the bass line, experimenting with rhythm patterns like this one:

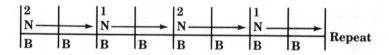

Notice that, with this rhythm pattern, the bass notes change every two beats, as in the basic pattern shown above.

3. During the white-note section of the piece, your ear will tell you that the melody gravitates toward this note:

To help orient your playing around this note, you might organize your melody around these notes:

Similarly, you may note that the center of musical gravity in the black-note section of the piece is this note:

You can organize your playing around these six black notes:

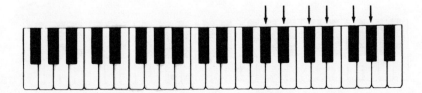

But if you want to get really fancy, you can throw in a few white notes during the black-note sections:

How's Tricks?

■ Well, that's the last trick up our sleeve, but there are hundreds of others you can discover on your own just by sitting down and experimenting with the tape. The next time someone asks you, "How's tricks?" be prepared to say: "Well, there's this one I found yesterday about . . ."

Chapter 8
Putting It All Together

A motion picture is pieced together from thousands of fragments of exposed film. By connecting the pieces, one to the other, the filmmaker creates a final product, complete with opening, main story, and ending. The piece is then one whole. How is a piece of music put together to form a whole? If you strip a piece of music down to its simplest parts, you come up with the same fundamental elements that serve as the building blocks of films and novels. A finished piece of music has a beginning, a middle, and an ending. Together they make up a complete song.

An Introduction to Introductions

■ Most pop songs, be they rockin' rave-ups or funky fingerpoppers or bluesy ballads, have introductions. An introduction is simply a short stretch of music that prepares you for the song to come. It gives you a chance to warm up and get some sense of what the song is going to sound like.

Most (but not all) of the pieces on the *Instant Piano* tape begin with introductions. What are they like? How do they work? Consider some of the pieces on Side 1 of the Instant Piano tape.

"Summer Mornings with You," the third song o[n] the tape, begins with four groups of notes that go h[igher and] higher in pitch. These notes communicate somethi[ng of the] sweet, sunny disposition of the song without being muc[h like the] rest of the piece. The introduction isn't a melody—it me[re]ates a mood.

The second song on Side 1, "Uptown Hoedown," begins with an introduction that does have its own melody, a little "Turkey in the Straw"-type ditty played on an electric guitar. This introduction is like a neon sign that flashes, I AM A COUNTRY AND WESTERN SONG.

What should *you* do with introductions? There are two options: If you think the introduction you hear on the tape is strong and sturdy enough to stand on its own, you can just sit back while it's playing. You can let it carry you and any listeners into the tune.

On the other hand, if you think an introduction you hear on the tape could benefit by adding your own playing to it, you can develop mini-melodies to begin these pieces.

Try This

1. Listen to the *Instant Piano* tape, trying as you do to identify the introductions to each piece on Side 1.

2. Return to the beginning of the tape and work on adding your own playing to each introduction. For example, see if you can devise a simple, buoyant melody to go along with the introduction to "Summer Mornings with You." Two or three notes might be all you need to both "sweeten" the introduction and to anticipate the type of melody you are likely to improvise during the body of the piece itself.

3. Once you've worked on introductions for the pieces on Side 1, move on to the pieces on Side 2. The same guidelines apply. Try to figure out what each piece really needs by way of introduction. Then ask yourself: Does the piece need more than is already supplied on the tape? If it does, you have your work cut out for you!

Making It to the Middle

■ Once you get past an introduction, you enter into a song's midsection, or middle. This is the main body of the song, the part that really *is* the piece. How are middles put together? Actually, they are made up of parts themselves.

Listen to "Summer Mornings with You," the third piece on Side 1 of the tape. If you've listened carefully you have probably noticed that after the introduction two distinct sections of music are played. Following the solo piano introduction, you hear a longish stretch of music in which the electric piano and drums play in a bright, easygoing fashion. This is the first, or A section.

At a certain point, the music changes; both the instruments and the quality of the sound change. The piano and drums continue to play, but you can also hear a cello repeating a simple melody. The music becomes a bit more tense and emotional—the sound darkens somewhat, as though a shadow has been cast on the sunlit scene painted in the A section. This darker section, with the cello, is the second, or B section.

Before long, the cello drops out and the music of the A section returns. This music sounds just like it did the first time around, except a bass can also be heard now.

After the repeat of the A section, the B section returns again, cello and all. Finally, the warming light of the A section repeats one last time. "Summer Mornings" has this structure:

Intro   A   B   A   B   A

Almost every pop song you hear uses some sort of A/B structure like the one above. AABA is another common form.

A/B is not the only possible arrangement, though. Some pieces on the *Instant Piano* tape have middles that consist of only one part repeated many times. On Side 1, "Blues in an Instant" has only one part to the middle section. The same is true of "Honky-Tonk Blues" and "Pachelbel's Canon" on Side 2.

When the main body of the piece is made up of repetitions of the same music, the musicians playing it have to work a little bit harder to keep the listener's interest. A performer will usually try to build the intensity of the piece with each subsequent repetition, until a climax is reached. There are many ways to do this. You can make the music progressively more complex with each repetition. Or, you can make the music louder, or faster, or higher in pitch as you go along, until sometime toward the end you've worked yourself into a screaming lather. You can then use the last repetition to cool out, slow down, ease your way out of the tune.

What do you do with the middles of songs? The best way to find out is by experimenting with the tunes themselves.

Try This

1. Play "Summer Mornings with You," the third song on Side 1. If you think it might help you follow the form of the piece, slip back to the diagram of its structure found on page 117. Improvise your way through the piece, noting when and where the changes between the A and B sections of the tune occur. Make your playing mirror the contrast between the two sections; during the A sections make your playing bright and relaxed. During the B sections, make your playing a bit edgier, more dramatic.

2. Improvise to one of the songs on the tape that has only one middle part. Each time a new repetition begins, change something about your playing. You can make these changes systematic or irregular. For example, you could begin playing on one group of five notes fairly low on the keyboard. When the first repetition begins, you could jump up to the next set of five notes, and then jump higher and higher on each subsequent repetition.

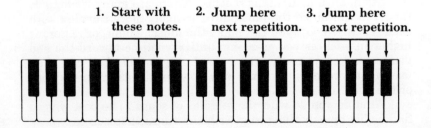

1. Start with these notes.   2. Jump here next repetition.   3. Jump here next repetition.

On each repetition, restrict yourself to the given five-note group. When you finish the piece, you should find yourself at the outer limits of the keyboard.

About Endings

■ The last thing to consider when putting a piece together is the ending. Like an introduction, an ending plays a vital but limited role in a piece of music. It gets you out of the piece and brings the performance to a satisfying conclusion.

Also like introductions, endings come in all shapes and sizes. Some are short and almost startling in their abruptness. A piece can simply stop, without preparation or advance warning. Other endings may be slow, protracted affairs—the piece may wind down or fade out, gradually getting softer and softer or slower and slower, or perhaps both. Between these two extremes—surprising stop or endless fade—lie the majority of endings you are likely to hear or play.

As you have probably noticed, most of the endings found on the *Instant Piano* tunes are compact and to the point. Some of the tunes, like "Summer Mornings with You," simply seem to stop at the end of a repeated A section. Others, like "Down in the Disco" (Side 1, Piece 1), end with a more or less literal repetition of the introduction. "Honky-Tonk Blues," on Side 2, ends with a little piece of music a musician would call a tag, something stuck on to the end of a piece to let you know it's over.

When you play with the pieces on the *Instant Piano* tape, use your ear to tell you when an ending is coming up so you can make the appropriate adjustments to your own playing. Essentially, this means being alert to the formal design of the piece and keeping track of its sections as you improvise your way through them.

Try This

1. Play along with "Summer Mornings with You" keeping track of the passing A and B sections. Note that the piece ends right after the A section is heard for the third time, just as you'd expect to move into another B section. Try to time your playing so that you end on the same beat as the taped music.

You might want to bring your performance of "Summer Mornings" to a close on one of these three notes:

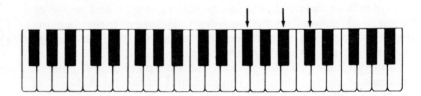

Ending on one of these notes will give your melody a sense of closure and finality—it won't feel as though your melody still has someplace it wants to go.

2. As for the endings to the rest of the pieces on the tape, work these out on your own. Remember that the way in which you end a piece is crucial to the way in which the entire piece will be perceived. If you end abruptly, without adequate preparation or resolution, the abrupt ending may be the thing a listener remembers most vividly about the piece. The same is true if you end delicately, carefully, easily. Neither way is "correct"—it depends entirely on your goals.

Putting It All Together

■ Beginnings, middles, endings—these fundamental elements, fleshed out with notes, harmonies, melodies, and bass lines are the things you must assemble to create a finished, complete piece of music. You can be very simple in what you play for each of these parts. The important thing is to create a piece of music that leads you—and any listeners—into the song, builds a main musical story, and then ends that story so no one is left hanging. A whole piece, rather than random, unconnected ramblings, even if it is rather rough in form, is one of the things that separates the sound of professional playing from amateur playing.

Chapter 9

You're on Your Own

Yd ou may thrill to recordings of the Brandenburg Concertos or tapes of a Jimi Hendrix concert, but in one crucial respect, your own playing has got to be better—just because it's your own. There is no substitute for the products of your own hands and your own imagination.

Up to this point, you have been reading about playing along with the *Instant Piano* tape. By improvising with it, you've discovered the joys of making music for yourself. Now it's time to take one . . . step . . . beyond. You're ready to take the training wheels off your bike. You can put aside the tape and make music that is entirely and uniquely your own.

Painting with Sound

■ One way to approach the piano when there are no accompaniments to back you up is to think of your playing as a painting.

Try This

1. Sit down and get comfortable at the keyboard. Take a few deep breaths. Clear your mind. Relax.

2. Put your right foot on your piano's sustain pedal, the one furthest to the right. Keep the pedal depressed through step 7 of this exercise.

3. With a finger on your right hand, play a black key near the center of the keyboard. You can lift your finger from the key and the note will continue to sound. Listen to the note as it fades. Think of it as a patch of color. What color is it when it first sounds? How does its color change as it fades?

Before the sound has faded away, strike a different black key with a finger on your left hand. Listen. Play a third note. Continue playing single notes with alternate hands, gradually playing faster until you are playing one note right after another. At the same time, gradually increase the volume of your playing. The density of the "sound mass" you are creating will increase slowly, until you have a thick fog of notes—like a painting smeared with many small daubs of paint.

4. When your "canvas" is covered with an opaque sheet of sound, undo the process. Gradually slow down and decrease the volume. End as you began, with a slow alternation of sustained notes.

5. Now set all ten fingers on black notes on the right side of the keyboard. Make sure you're still stepping on the sustain pedal. Flutter your fingers up and down, striking the notes in a random sequence. Play rapidly but gently. Try to create a gossamer, shimmering sound, the sound of a thousand butterfly wings fluttering at once.

6. Stop playing and let these high, thin notes ring. Shift your body and your hands to the middle of the keyboard. Flutter lightly on another group of black notes.

Start playing softly and slowly. Build both the volume and the speed of your fluttering until you've whipped up a raging torrent of sound. Stop suddenly and listen as the torrent subsides.

7. Now play black notes on the left side of the keyboard. Keep the pedal down. Beginning with the little finger on your left hand, roll your fingers up the keyboard, from left to right. Do it slowly at first to get the feel of it; left 5 (pinky)-4-3-2-1 (thumb), right 1 (thumb)-2-3-4-5-(pinky). Let your hand move up a little and roll again. Keep rolling up the keyboard. Then try rolling back down; lift your foot off the pedal.

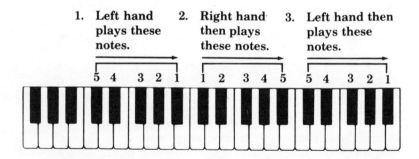

1. **Left hand plays these notes.**
2. **Right hand then plays these notes.**
3. **Left hand then plays these notes.**

Pound That Piano

The same way an artist can apply almost invisible, feathery touches of color or can throw an entire can of paint at the canvas, the improviser can tickle the keys or pound them.

Try This

1. Put your foot back on the pedal and keep it there. Now try playing using your whole hand, stretched out flat and held parallel to the keyboard, as if you were getting ready to play a bongo drum. Start with your right hand. The side of your thumb should be facing you and the side of your pinky facing the piano.

2. Strike a large group of black notes. Keep your hand in one position relative to the keyboard, so that it always strikes the same group of notes, and use it to beat out simple rhythms. You might imagine yourself playing a bongo drum with one hand. "Drum" in other regions of the keyboard.

3. Try "drumming" with two hands. You can alternate between left and right hands, or you can make up more complex patterns.

Swept Away

A popular piano technique is a long stretched-out sound that can suggest the landing or takeoff of a jumbo jet. Here's how to paint that swept-away sound.

Try This

1. Keep the sustain pedal depressed. Set the *back* of your right index finger on a group of low black notes. Sweep your hand up along the black notes, moving left to right, and bearing down hard enough to make the notes sound. (Don't press *too* hard, or you may chafe your skin.)

A more comfortable way to do this is to use the palm of your hand. Try to cover the entire keyboard.

2. Now sweep down the black notes from right to left. You should be getting a gliding, harplike sound.

3. Experiment with sweeping up and down the piano this way. Sweep at different speeds. Sweep up several times in a row, in rapid succession. Sweep down in the same way. Then alternate rapidly between upward sweeps and downward sweeps.

4. Sweep up and down along shorter segments of the keyboard instead of along its entire length. You can do this by sweeping from your wrist, as if you were dusting with a feather duster.

5. Sweep with two hands, with the palms of both hands sweeping in the same direction as if wiping away dust. Sweep in opposite directions, with both hands near the center of the keyboard. Sweep with alternate hands. Let yourself be swept away.

The Image of Melody

Some musicians "see things." They imagine pictures in their heads and play what they see.

Try This

1. Play single-note melodies—the kind you play when you play with the *Instant Piano* tape—but keep the sustain pedal depressed. Note how the use of the pedal can affect the color and mood of a melody. Try to exploit the pedal's effects. What sorts of images or moods does a sustained melody suggest?

2. Try to play with specific images in mind. Play like a shepherd in a high mountain meadow, tootling on a home-made flute as he tends his flock. Play the sound of church bells heard from a great distance. Play the sound of a bugler blowing reveille at dawn. Play the sound of a lone violinist in an almost empty subway station. Let your understanding of melody-making help you use the pedal to create rich, evocative sounds.

3. Imagine yourself to be watching a movie, with your playing providing the soundtrack. Turn the images you have been improvising into a full-length feature movie. Such a story will probably consist of several sections, each with its own mood and action. When you play the story, you can use contrasting musical elements to distinguish between and characterize each of the sections.

For example, how would you play an ascent of Mount Everest? Think of the long, slow plod up sheer, snowy, windblown cliffs. Imagine the intense, almost religious exhilaration you would feel as you reached the top—the top of the world. Then the treacherous but anticlimactic descent—what would your mood be then? How would you express it musically?

Keep in mind that there is no right way to tell a story in music. You can't relate a story in music with the precision that words allow, so your descriptions will always be approximate and inexact. At the same time, though, you may find it possible to express emotions and images musically that words alone could never do justice to. Musical expression and evocation is the work of imagination—let yours run untethered when you play.

4. If you have a hard time sustaining a scene or story in your imagination *and* playing at the same time, you may want to try this: Put a television in a spot where you can see it while sitting at the piano. Turn the set on, find a show or movie that looks interesting, and turn down the sound. Use the black and/or white keys and play along as if you were providing the soundtrack. Imagine yourself to be playing for an audience of viewers who are relying on your accompaniment to clue them in to what's happening on the screen. Is the elegantly dressed couple squabbling or making up? Is the skinny guy telling a bad joke to a group of offended strangers, or is he delivering sad news to his family? Is the show a sitcom, a docudrama, a biblical epic, a soap opera, or a war story? Use your "painting" skills to alert your imaginary audience to the nature of the show and to changes in its mood and action. With the sound turned down, you *yourself* may not know what's going on, so you'll have to use your imagination. Use your music to imbue the television's flickering images with meanings that *you* choose.

Beyond Painting

■ Painting with sound is great fun, and it's a wonderful way to create colorful, expressive music when playing on your own. It's likely, though, that you're starting to want more; you want to make music that sounds more like music you usually listen to, music with rhythm and melody and harmony and a bass line.

A good way to get started making this kind of music on your own is to work with bass lines. A bass line is simply a sequence of notes, played down low on the piano, that provides the foundation for the music. The melody, which is played above, can be thought to sit on the bass line, the way a house sits on a basement. Bass lines usually follow repeated patterns. These patterns often hold a piece together, giving it structure, organization, and a feeling of motion and change.

One-Note Bass Lines

In the next set of exercises, you will experiment with simple procedures for making one-note bass lines.

Try This

1. You can make a simple but effective bass line out of one note played in a regular rhythmic pattern. You're probably better off if you do not use the pedal, since sustaining the sound of the bass note often creates a muddy effect. Begin by playing this note in the bass, somewhere in the bottom third of the keyboard:

Play it repeatedly, using one of the following rhythm patterns, or make up one of your own. You can keep the beat by tapping one foot.

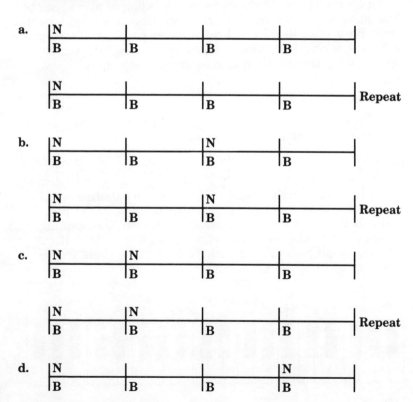

2. Once you can play the bass line steadily, using your chosen rhythm, play a melody with your right hand on the black notes. Keep it simple—a few notes, repeated, would do fine for a start. As you grow more confident, you can vary the rhythm of the bass and increase the complexity of your melody. Don't rush it. Just take it easy.

3. Shift your one-note bass line to this note:

Keep playing a repeated rhythmic pattern in the bass and making melodies with your right hand on the black notes. Does the change in the bass note change the character of your melody in some way? Can you describe the change?

Two-Note Bass Lines

A one-note bass line is fine—for a while. It soon becomes monotonous, however, even if you change its rhythm. This is because the bass note determines to a great degree the color or feeling of the melody it underpins. An unchanging bass line can make your melodies sound monochromatic and emotionally flat. So the trick is to change your bass note every now and then, depending upon how, and how often, you want the color of the melody to shift. In most music, the bass notes change at fixed, repeated intervals—every eight beats, say, or every four.

Try This

   1. To begin with, make a two-note bass line using the two notes shown below. Play the first note and hold it for four beats. Then play the second note and hold *it* for four beats. Shift back to the first—and so on.

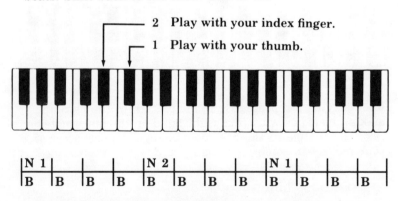

   Once you get the hang of the pattern, add some right-hand melody on the black notes. Keep your playing slow and steady. Ease into the fancier stuff.

2. Try making different patterns with the two bass notes, or make up two-note bass lines out of other pairs of notes. Here are a few good choices.

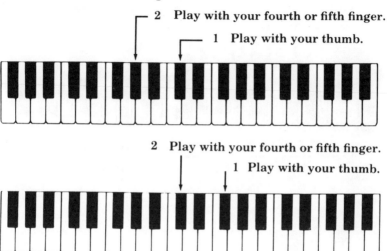

2 Play with your fourth or fifth finger.

1 Play with your thumb.

2 Play with your fourth or fifth finger.

1 Play with your thumb.

Multi-Note Bass Lines

Try some multi-note bass lines. The notes in each pattern and the order in which they are played are shown. A suggested anchor finger is also given. (Your pinky is 5 and your thumb is 1.) Keep the anchor finger resting lightly on the note shown or stay close to it at all times. That way your other fingers will be in a good position to play the different bass notes, and you won't have to hop around the keyboard looking for them.

1.

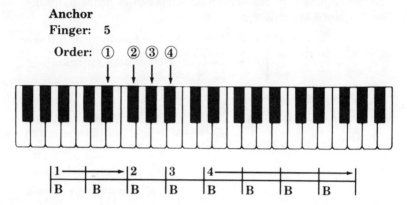

Anchor Finger: 5

Order: ① ④ ② ③

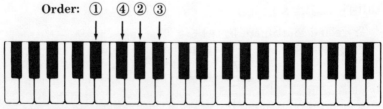

See rhythm pattern below.

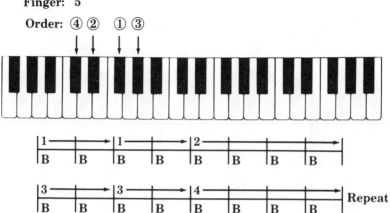

2.

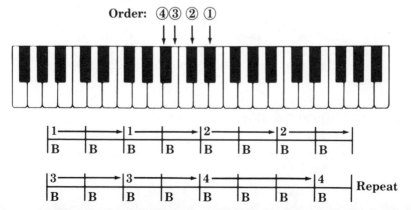

3.

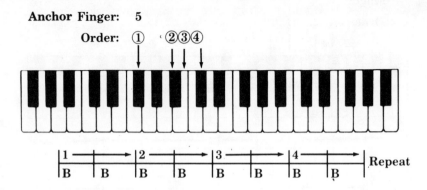

Anchor Finger: 5

Order: ① ②③④

1 ——→ | 2 ——→ | 3 ——→ | 4 ——→ | Repeat

B | B | B | B | B | B | B | B

4. Make sure you have the bass line "in your fingers" before adding melody to it. When you do start adding melodies on the black notes, keep them simple. Your main concern should be to keep the bass line chugging along steadily and to keep your melody in synch rhythmically with the bass line. Be sure also to make up some bass lines of your own.

Connecting Bass Lines

Okay, your bass lines are becoming more complex—but they still repeat at very short intervals. This doesn't make for a dynamic musical structure. What to do?

In earlier exercises, you used contrast to create pieces with distinctive dramatic structures. In the same way, you can use contrasts between bass lines to give a piece a sense of motion and change. In essence, this means simply moving from one bass line to another. Each bass line has its own unique feeling or color, so shifting between two or more bass lines helps give a piece a sense of dynamic ebb and flow.

Try This

1. To begin with, try linking two 2-note bass lines in a repeating series. For example, start with the bass line that alternates between these two notes.

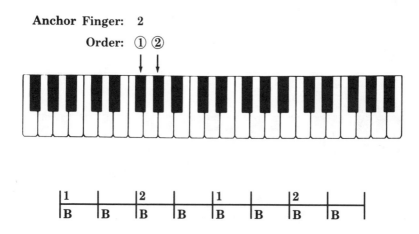

Anchor Finger: 2

Order: ① ②

The second line alternates between these two notes:

Anchor
Finger: 5

Order: ③ ④

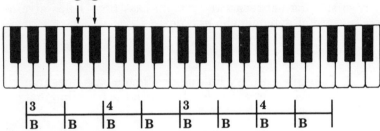

Put the two together and you get a pattern like this:

Anchor
Finger: 4

Order: ③ ④ ① ②

2. Keep repeating this entire pattern and you wind up with a piece that consists of two (short) alternating sections. To heighten the sense of contrast between these two sections, you can play each individual section longer before switching back to the other. For example, you could play the one-two section for sixteen beats, instead of eight, and then play the three-four section for sixteen beats before switching back.

3. You can jazz up this bass line by changing its rhythm. For example, you can play a single rhythm throughout, like this:

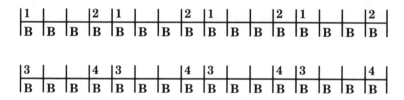

4. You can also use a different rhythm for each section:

5. Begin to experiment with different combinations of bass lines. There are, obviously, innumerable possibilities. We could show you more—in fact, we could fill several volumes with interesting bass lines—but you'll probably find it more rewarding to make up your own. You may find it helpful, as you do, to make keyboard illustrations like those shown above to help you keep track of the notes you want to play, the order in which you want to play them, and the fingering you find most comfortable.

6. Whenever you begin playing a new bass line, keep your playing slow and steady and your melodies simple. As you learn to play the bass line automatically, your melodies will begin to flower naturally. Take your time—don't rush into things you can't quite handle. Let your motto be "one thing at a time."

Blues Bass Line

Before we finish with bass lines, there is one rather special bass line we'd like to show you, the bass line for the blues. When musicians say they want to play the blues, they are referring to a fixed bass line formula that, in the course of any blues performance, will be repeated many times. Below are two very basic versions of the blues. These lines are somewhat longer than those you are accustomed to, but with a little practice they should fall easily under your fingers.

1.

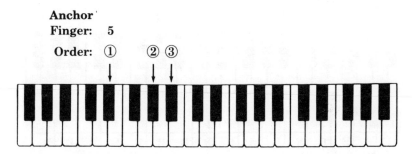

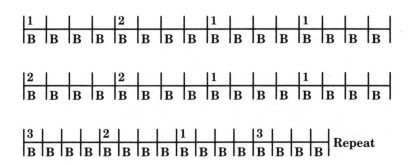

2.

Anchor Finger: 5

Order: ① ② ③

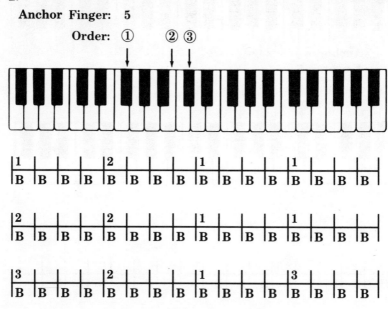

3. Practice these patterns until you have them almost memorized. That will make it a lot easier for you to play along with the right hand. When you do get around to adding melody on the black notes to your performance of the blues, be sure to fool around with the "blue notes" you learned about in Chapter 5. For the first blues bass line shown above, the extra white notes you can experiment with are:

For the second bass line, the blues notes are:

Playing the blues can easily become an addictive past-time—and it's one addiction you might want to cultivate. For all its simplicity, the blues is a musical structure whose expressive possibilities seem inexhaustible, and whose popularity, with both musicians and music lovers, is universal. Now, you are prepared to join the ranks of both the blues lovers and the blues players. Yeah, man, play the blues.

Freestyle

One final thought: Your bass lines need not follow fixed patterns. It's perfectly acceptable to play bass lines that wander all over the place without ever retracing any paths. You might want to try playing this way.

Try This

1. Set a slow, even beat and play one different bass note per beat. Don't think—let your fingers find their own way. The result should be a slinky, jazzy, walking bass line.

2. If you accentuate the notes you play on every second and fourth beat, you will exaggerate the jazziness of the line. Try it and see.

Because a walking bass line is, by definition, always in motion, your melodies need not move much. In fact, you might find that the most swinging music you make consists of a serpentine walking bass line combined with a spare, stripped-down, blues-tinged melody, a melody made from just one or two carefully chosen notes.

Making It on Your Own

You've now explored two very different ways of making music on your own. Using the techniques for "painting," you can make impressionistic musical renderings of scenes, stories, and emotions. Using bass lines, you can make pieces that have distinctive musical and dramatic shapes, pieces that are more like songs than "aural paintings."

How far you go with each of these techniques is up to you. As you explore the world of sound painting, you may begin to devise your own unique expressive devices and technical tricks. As you do, you may find yourself able to reproduce images and evoke moods with an almost uncanny realism—listeners may know at once what it is you are attempting to communicate.

As you experiment with bass lines, you will find yourself creating ever more sophisticated musical structures. Your pieces will have clearly audible shapes and forms, which you will be able to adjust for maximum expressive and dramatic effect.

If you are patient, willing to take chances, willing to make mistakes, ready to rip the shackles off of your imagination, if you love what you're doing, love both mucking around with the nitty-gritty details of music-making and taking in its sweeping vistas, if you can go slow, take it easy, keep it simple, relax, then all these good things—and many more—can easily happen. You can make music—beautiful, rich, emotional music—and you can do it on your own.

Chapter 10

Coming Attractions

The preceding chapters and the music on the *Instant Piano* tape have given you a sneak preview, a glimpse of what it's really like to be a musician. You've been able to achieve sounds and improvise at a level that usually isn't reached until after several years of lessons. You've had the experience of knowing what many professionals feel when they can just play music without having to think about what they're doing.

Despite that experience, some of you are ready to move on to other things. Remember that *Instant Piano* is always there for you to "mess around with" and give you a quick jolt of fun and relaxation. The rest of you have discovered the power of music and are ready to move deeper into the wonderful worlds of jazz, rock, pop, classical, country, rhythm and blues . . . This chapter is for you. The following suggestions will give you an idea of the coming attractions and what you can do to make your musical experience more exciting and fulfilling.

Learn the Language

■ If your passion is Debussy and Chopin, you will have to learn to read music. Almost all classical music is written out, and most of it is far too complicated to learn to play by ear. But even if you want to play jazz or rock, a knowledge of music notation will simplify your life and help you to "dope out" songs quickly and easily. There are many self-instructional materials, as well as aids like flash cards and keyboard charts, available in stores.

What's Behind It All?

■ There really is a method to the madness of music, a rhyme and reason behind the notes, beats, and chords. If you understand the basic concepts of music, you will be able to apply them to anything you play or want to play. You will begin to see the same patterns cropping up again and again and thus you can anticipate them in your playing. A good theory book will tell you what you need to know. In it you'll discover everything from the names of notes and chords, to how to count beats, to what those funny little marks mean on the sheet music you're trying to interpret.

Listen! Listen! Listen!

■ Educated ears are essential to successful music-making. Send yours to school every day and make sure they do their homework. Listen to all kinds of music on radio or stereo—classical, pop, rhythm and blues—anything that turns you on. Listen to it, dance to it, sing with it, play along. Go out where you can hear music played live. Fill your ears with sound. The more good music you put inside you the more will eventually come out in your playing.

Play! Play! Play!

■ Probably the only thing more valuable than listening to people making music is getting in there and making it yourself. Look around, find as many people as you can, get together as often as possible, and play. You can learn more about music from playing and sharing with your peers than you can from any teacher or any book.

Have Fun

■ There's no getting away from it—true mastery of any art is hard work. In the weeks, months, or years to come, whenever you begin to find the work overwhelming and the joy has gone out of your playing, come back to *Instant Piano* and just have fun. Get back to the most crucial aspect of music-making: self-expression. Let loose, let yourself go, and discover all over again the incredible range of emotions and imagination you can unleash at the keyboard. Hear yourself say once more what all children know: "I love to play!"

Appendix A

How *Instant Piano* Works

If you already know a thing or two about music theory, you've probably guessed why *Instant Piano* works, why it's possible to play along with the tape using just the black notes with Side 1 and just the white notes on Side 2.

While we wish that this was a deep, dark, secret, it simply isn't. *Instant Piano* works according to a very simple principle:

All of the pieces on Side 1 of the *Instant Piano* tape are played in the keys of G♭ major, E♭ minor, or, in the case of "Blues in an Instant," E♭ major. When you play on the black notes of the piano, you are actually playing a pentatonic five-note scale whose notes are all members of the major, minor, or blues scale ordinarily associated with those three keys. So when you play a piece written in one of these keys, playing on the black notes ensures that you won't hit a wrong note—every note you play will either be a scale tone, or a chord tone, or both.

Side 2 works in a similar fashion. On this side of the tape, all of the pieces are in the keys of either C major or A minor, or, in the case of "Honky-Tonk Blues," A major. When you play just the white notes of the piano, you automatically play in either C major or A minor. If you leave out the notes F and B, as suggested in some places, you wind up with another pentatonic scale. Once again, the notes of this scale will blend nicely with any of the three tonalities used on Side 2.

See? It's as easy as that. There's really no mystery at all.

Appendix B
Chord Progressions

Below are the chord progressions for the A and B sections of each piece on *Instant Piano*. The introductions and endings are shown where applicable. The order in which the sections repeat differs on each piece. Listen to the tape for the exact order of repetition. The following songs are all in common time (four beats per measure with the quarter note equalling one beat).

"Down in the Disco" (Side 1, Piece 1)

	G♭maj7	A♭m7	G♭maj7	A♭m7
Intro	/ / / /	/ / / /	/ / / /	/ / / /

	G♭maj7	A♭m7	G♭maj7	A♭m7
A	/ / / /	/ / / /	/ / / /	/ / / /

| B♭m7 | A♭m7 | B♭m7 |
| / / / / | / / / / | / / / / |

| 1. A♭m7 D♭ | 2. C♭maj7 D♭ |
| / /   / / | / /   / / |

B

| E♭m | B♭m7 | E♭m | B♭m7 |
| / / / / | / / / / | / / / / | / / / / |

| A♭m7 | B♭m7 | C♭maj7 | D♭sus4   D♭ |
| / / / / | / / / / | / / / / | / /   / / |

Ending

| G♭maj7 | C♭maj7 | G♭maj7 | C♭maj7 |
| / / / / | / / / / | / / / / | / / / / |

| G♭maj7 | C♭maj7 | G♭maj7 |
| / / / / | / / / / | / / / / |

"Uptown Hoedown" (Side 1, Piece 2)

Intro
| F♯ | F♯ C♯ |
| / / / / | / / / / |

A
| F♯ | B | F♯ | C♯ |
| / / / / | / / / / | / / / / | / / / / |

| F♯ | B | F♯ C♯ |
| / / / / | / / / / | / / / / |

1.	2.
F♯ C♯	F♯ F♯7
/ / / /	/ / / /

B
| B | F♯ | C♯ | F♯ F♯7 |
| / / / / | / / / / | / / / / | / / / / |

| B | F♯ | C♯ | F♯ C♯ |
| / / / / | / / / / | / / / / | / / / / |

Ending
| F♯ | F♯ F♯ C♯ F♯ |
| / / / / | / / / / / |

"Summer Mornings with You" (Side 1, Piece 3)

Intro
| G♭maj7 | A♭m7 | G♭maj7 | A♭m7 |
| / / / / | / / / / | / / / / | / / / / |

A
| G♭maj7   A♭m7 | B♭m7   A♭m7 | G♭   A♭m7 |
| / /   / / | / /   / / | / /   / / |

| B♭m7   A♭m7 | G♭maj7   A♭m7 | B♭m7   A♭m7 |
| / /   / / | / /   / / | / /   / / |

| G♭maj7   A♭m7 | B♭m7   C♭   D♭ |
| / /   / / | / /   /   / |

B
| E♭m | E | E♭m | E |
| / / / / | / / / / | / / / / | / / / / |

| E♭m | E | G♭   C♭ | D♭sus   D♭ |
| / / / / | / / / / | / /   / / | / /   / / |

117

"Breakin' Out" (Side 1, Piece 4)

Intro (Drum Solo)

A
| E♭m / / / / | E♭m / / / / | D♭ / / / / | D♭ / / / / |

| C♭ / / / / | D♭ / / / / | E♭m / / / / | E♭m / / / / |

B
| E♭m / / / / | E♭m / / / / | D♭ / / / / | D♭ / / / / |

| E♭m / / / / | E♭m / / / / | D♭ / / / / | D♭ / / / / |

| C♭ / / / / | D♭ / / / / | E♭m / / / / | E♭m / / / / |

"Blues in an Instant" (Side 1, Piece 5)

Intro

| Eb | Gb7 | Fm7 | E7 | Eb | Gb | Fm7 | Bb7 |
| / / | / / | / / | / / | / / | / / | / / | / / |

| Eb7 | Ab7 | Eb7 | Eb7 |
| / / / / | / / / / | / / / / | / / / / |

| Ab7 | Ab7 | Eb7 | Eb7 |
| / / / / | / / / / | / / / / | / / / / |

| Fm7 | Bb7 | Eb7 C7 | Fm7 Bb7 |
| / / / / | / / / / | / / / / | / / / / |

"Pushy" (Side 1, Piece 6)

Intro | E♭m | E♭m | C♭ | C♭ |
         | / / / / | / / / / | / / / / | / / / / |

         | D♭ | D♭ | E♭m | E♭m |
         | / / / / | / / / / | / / / / | / / / / |

A | E♭m | E♭m | C♭ | C♭ |
         | / / / / | / / / / | / / / / | / / / / |

         | D♭ | D♭ | E♭m | E♭m |
         | / / / / | / / / / | / / / / | / / / / |

B | A♭m | A♭m | E♭m | E♭m |
         | / / / / | / / / / | / / / / | / / / / |

         | A♭m | A♭m | E♭m | E♭m |
         | / / / / | / / / / | / / / / | / / / / |

         | A♭m | A♭m | E♭m | E♭m |
         | / / / / | / / / / | / / / / | / / / / |

$$\left|\ \text{A♭m}\ /\ /\ /\ /\ \left|\ \text{G♭}\quad\text{B♭}\ /\ /\ /\ /\ \left|\ \text{D♭sus}\ /\ /\ /\ /\ \left|\ \text{D♭}\ /\ /\ /\ /\ \right|\right.\right.\right.$$

C
$$\left|\ \text{E♭m}\ /\ /\ /\ /\ \left|\ \text{E♭m}\ /\ /\ /\ /\ \left|\ \text{C♭}\ /\ /\ /\ /\ \left|\ \text{C♭}\ /\ /\ /\ /\ \right|\right.\right.\right.$$

$$\left|\ \text{D♭}\ /\ /\ /\ /\ \left|\ \text{D♭}\ /\ /\ /\ /\ \left|\ \text{E♭m}\ /\ /\ /\ /\ \left|\ \text{E♭m}\ /\ /\ /\ /\ \right|\right.\right.\right.$$

"Jump Rock" (Side 2, Piece 1)

A
| C / / / / | F / / / / | C / / / / | F / / / / |

| C / / / / | F / / / / | C / / / / | F / / / / |

| G / / / / | G / / / / | F / / / / | F / / / / |

| G / / / / | G / / / / | F / / / / | F/G / / / / |

| C / / / / | F / / / / | C / / / / | F / / / / |

| C / / / / | F / / / / | C / / / / | F / / / / |

B
| Am / / / / | G / / / / | F / / / / | F   G / / / / |

| Am / / / / | G / / / / | F / / / / | F / / / / |

"Canon in C à la Pachelbel" (Side 2, Piece 2)

Repeated for entire piece

C	G	Am	Em	F	C	F	G
/ /	/ /	/ /	/ /	/ /	/ /	/ /	/ /

"Fifties Rock" (Side 2, Piece 3)

Intro | C   F | C   G |
         | / / / / | / / / / |

A | C | G | Am | F |
         | / / / / | / / / / | / / / / | / / / / |

         | C | G |
         | / / / / | / / / / |

         1.
         | C   F | C   G |
         | / / / / | / / / / |

         2.
         | C   F | C   C7 |
         | / / / / | / / / / |

B | F | C | G | C   C7 |
         | / / / / | / / / / | / / / / | / / / / |

         | F | C | D7 | G7 |
         | / / / / | / / / / | / / / / | / / / / |

124

"'Lectronic Lady" (Side 2, Piece 4)

A
| Am / / / / | Am / / / / | Am / / / / | Am / / / / |

| Am / / / / | Am / / / / | Am / / / / | Am / / / / |

| F / / / / | F / / / / | Am / / / / | Am / / / / |

| F / / / / | F / / / / | Am / / / / | Am / / / / |

B
| Dm / / / / | Dm / / / / | Am / / / / | Am / / / / |

| Dm / / / / | Dm / / / / | Am / / / / | Am / / / / |

| G / / / / | G / / / / | Am / / / / | Am / / / / |

| G / / / / | G / / / / | Am / / / / | Am / / / / |

"Honky-Tonk Blues" (Side 2, Piece 5)

Intro
```
| A      D/A     A      D/A  | A      E7      |
| /      /       /      /    | / /    / /     |
```

A
```
|   A7        |   D7        |   A7        |   A7        |
| / / / /     | / / / /     | / / / /     | / / / /     |

|   D7        |   D7        |   A7        |   A7        |
| / / / /     | / / / /     | / / / /     | / / / /     |

|   E7        |   D7        |   A7        | A      E7   |
| / / / /     | / / / /     | / / / /     | / /    / /  |
```

126

"Just Before Dawn" (Side 2, Piece 6)

"Switch!" (Side 2, Piece 7)

A
$$\left|\begin{array}{cc} \text{G} & \text{F} \\ / / & / / \end{array}\right|$$

(Repeats 8 times, alternating with B section.)

B
$$\left|\begin{array}{cc} \text{A\flat m7} & \text{D\flat 7} \\ / / & / / \end{array}\right|$$

(Repeats 8 times, alternating with A section.)

Appendix C
How to Use with Other Instruments

Okay, so you're not a piano player, and you're not interested in becoming one—you play the bassoon, let's say. Or maybe you don't have a piano, but you do have a guitar. Or maybe you play the piano, but you have a friend who plays the trumpet. Will *Instant Piano* work with these instruments, too?

Of course, it's easy. You simply need to do three things:

1. Get a fingering chart for your instrument. This is a chart that will tell you how to find and finger all of the notes your instrument is capable of producing. (If you already are able to find notes on your instrument, you can skip this step.)

2. To play along with the pieces on Side 1 of the *Instant Piano* tape, you only need to find five notes:

G♭, A♭, B♭, D♭, E♭

(You will have to play these notes at concert pitch. If you don't know what this means, consult your method book or your teacher.)

Once you have found these notes, you can play with Side 1. Remember, you may use these notes in all of the registers your instrument can reach. Read *Instant Piano* to find out just what you should do with these notes once you've found them!

3. To play along with the pieces on Side 2 of the *Instant Piano* tape, you need to find and play these five notes (concert pitch):

C, D, E, G, A

In some places, you will also be able to use F and B. But when getting started, stick to the five-note scale on Side 2. It will make your life easier.

That's all there is to it. Armed with these two groups of five notes, you should be ready to conquer *Instant Piano*. Forward, march!